A Joyful Heart

A JOYFUL HEART

Meditations for Lent

MARTIN THORNTON

COWLEY

Published in Great Britain by S.P.C.K.
Published in the United States of America by Cowley Publications.

International Standard Book No.: 0-936384-45-X
Cover design by Sylvia N. Slayton

Cowley Publications
980 Memorial Drive
Cambridge, MA 02138

MARTIN THORNTON
1915 - 1986

I will turn their mourning into joy,
I will comfort them, and give them gladness for sorrow.
—Jer. 31:13

To Magdalen Mary
with all my love

Contents

1

Preface for Pancake Day

'Lightsome – graceful, cheerful, bright, luminous, enlivening, clear, manifest . . .'

G. K. Chesterton revived the tradition of treating theology, that most serious of all studies, as light-heartedly as possible; nothing frivolous, certainly not impious, but as a sensibly humble approach to divine mystery. I think it was Father F. C. Copleston (if not, it was someone of similar eminence) who described Chesterton's little study of St Thomas Aquinas as the most brilliantly lucid exposition of what Thomism stood for. It is also very funny.

More recently C. S. Lewis has continued in this tradition; Screwtape is also very funny while presenting the most subtle depths of orthodox moral theology. It is all seriously pastoral – lightsome, luminous, enlightening.

I have been careful to speak of the revival of tradition, not the invention of something outside it, more especially the tradition of Christian spirituality. In 1681 the Anglican divine, Anthony Horneck, published a devotional work ('Lent book'?) called *The Happy Ascetic*. Many will be familiar with the deeply devout optimism of Julian of Norwich, whose writing is currently so popular. As far back as the second century of our era the author of the *Shepherd of Hermas* exhorted any who would take prayer seriously to 'clothe thyself with cheerfulness . . . cleanse thyself from this wicked sadness, and thou shalt live unto God'. Perhaps there is some subtle significance in the fact that one of the most renowned of all medieval mystical classics is called the *Divine Comedy*.

Chesterton and others have argued that the perfect humanity of Jesus had to embrace a sense of humour, the lightsomeness of Christ who, on a most solemn occasion, joked about camels walking through eyes of needles. (Must scholars explain it away and spoil the joke?) All the disciples wanted after a fruitless night's fishing was a modest breakfast, not a hundred and fifty-three whoppers that broke the nets and flooded the boat. All the

1

bride's father needed was a further half-dozen of plonk, not a hundred and twenty gallons of heavenly vintage. The woman at the well, the woman taken in adultery, St Peter's attempt to walk on the water; in these and other stories Jesus dealt with the most serious of truths and principles, but laced them with the divine sense of humour.

It would be foolhardy for me, or anyone else, to try to emulate these devotional masters of the lightsome idiom, cheaply to ape the genius of Chesterton and Lewis, but it seems permissible, on pancake day, to accept the tradition and look forward to Lent with a devotionally light heart; to seek the superlative joys of penitence, forgiveness, discipline and prayer. Nearer to home, I remember Dr Margaret Hewitt introducing her series of lectures in Truro Cathedral with an exhortation to give up gloom for Lent.

Baron von Hügel popularized the word *attrait*, the penchant, inclination, attraction for, particular forms of prayer or approaches to spirituality, consistent with the unique make-up of individual people. There is tremendous strength in the harshness of such classics as the *Imitation of Christ* or the writings of a William Law. There is also a sublime devotional power in St Thérèse of Lisieux, but none of these schools of devotion is right for everyone, and there is nothing to be ashamed of if they fail to speak to an individual Christian; it is a question of *attrait*. It is the same with the lightsome mood, it is not for everyone; here my only apologia is that it is a legitimate approach, embedded in the tradition, and one that may possibly be due for revival.

There are dangers on all sides; there always are. The sternness of some medieval writing can lead to despair, an exaggerated affective or emotional approach can end in senti- mentality. The approach here suggested also has its weak- nesses. Chesterton has been accused of making his Christianity far too cosy, his stress is on the glories of creation and the wonder of incarnation, with, some would say, too little emphasis on the passion and the cross. One may rightly extol the joyful glory of divine forgiveness and revel in the privilege of sacramental absolution, but you cannot be light-hearted about sin. Lewis also deeply offended some by looking at things from the devil's side and referring to God as the Enemy. In what follows I have no wish to give offence to anyone, or to bring in profanity for cheap effect, yet I foresee some danger in my analogical interpretation of the incarnation and the Trinity in terms of lobsters and woodlice. My defence is that the analogy plainly impressed on a former, live occasion.

To be even more personal, for a pancake-day preface, I would explain that this year 1987 marks the centenary of the consecration of Truro Cathedral, in which I was privileged to serve as Canon Chancellor for ten years. I have no certain record as to how many sermons, lectures, devotional addresses and miscellaneous talks I delivered during that period: but at a rough guess and for present assessment the round figure of a thousand should not be far out. From the viewpoint of retirement, with no more axes to grind or excuses to make, one might speculate on the sort of impact all this talking made. It is probably more or less consistent with the careers of most other clergymen in any other place after a ten-year pastoral stint. It would be safe to say that some 95 per cent or 950 out of 1000 such talks were received with varying degrees of interest and attention, dismissed after an hour or two and forgotten next day. The lectures were dutifully attended by candidates for ordination, absorbed and annotated, to form the basis of a boring and generally useless exercise of trying to pass examinations.

In my case around 4 per cent, or 40 out of the 1000 had sufficient force to arouse positive opposition. I remain sincerely grateful to the more forthcoming and perspicacious section of the cathedral congregation for giving vent to such healthy opposition: 'What was the matter with Martin today? Hangover or something? It was awful.' 'Excuse me, Father, but really that was rubbish, all waffle and cliché.' That is so much healthier than apathy.

And then there were ten. One per cent which might, with all the reservation associated by the word in this context, be acclaimed as 'successful'. Just once a year there may be a time when the preacher or lecturer simply knows, with thanksgiving, that the Holy Spirit has been working overtime, when it has come off, when there is a tangible rapport between preacher and congregation, lecturer and audience. The 4 per cent group of intelligent critics might even become congratulatory. The content of this Lent book consists in a reworking of these few highlights, if one such per year is not too generous a claim; a reworking of a few basic themes presented in light-hearted analogy and home-spun parable, then welded into some sort of lenten pattern. At least the book may claim the advantage of being grounded in pastoral experience, in a presentation which has by the grace of God aroused interest, if only within the narrow compass of the curious Cornish.

To summarize both approach and foundation: when the general idea of this Lent book came fairly into view I mentioned its possibilities to various friends in Truro; colleagues, layfolk, choristers, schoolgirls. I tried to explain the light-hearted yet underlying seriousness of the Chesterton–Lewis idiom: does a Lent book have to be either grim or sloppy? The response was spontaneous and consistent, with the schoolgirls leading the chorus: 'What you mean', they all replied, 'is the Woodlouse Sermon.' Precisely what special qualities there were in the Woodlouse Sermon I cannot explain, only the analogy itself claims anything like originality, but modesty apart a sermon actually remembered by schoolgirls after several years must have something about it. On this occasion at least the opening prayer seems to have been accepted by the Blessed Trinity, the Holy Spirit must have been especially active. I had just been to confession so maybe grace was flowing more freely than usual, perhaps the delivery was curiously above standard. The devastating thing is that after a ten-year slog, doing my poor best in cathedral and diocese, having responsibility for five groups of ordination candidates, organizing three long courses on spiritual direction, giving my thousand talks of various sorts and playing my most incompetent part in general administration: after all this and more, where he is not wholly forgotten, Chancellor Thornton is remembered for the Woodlouse Sermon. The frightening query and gigantic risk is how this sort of thing will stand up to its traumatic translation into print. Perhaps it is worth the risk.

The customary purpose of a Lent book is to stimulate meditative insight into the great mysteries of the faith, thus to help deepen and expand the reader's life of prayer. I take prayer to mean the working out of our total, continuous, unbreakable relation with God in Christ, freely given in baptism. Prayer is not an exercise we occasionally perform but a response to a status in which we are. It implies obedience to a covenanted relation with God the Father, a living encounter with the Son, and finally incorporation into the sacred humanity of Jesus through the Holy Spirit. Prayer is both objective and subjective, giving and receiving; both are appropriate so long as we get them in balance and the right way round. Prayer is both corporate yet intensely personal (later the cricket analogy, in chapter 6, might help), so to separate personal devotion from public worship is to make a false distinction: their inter-relation is essential.

Nevertheless it is generally assumed that a Lent book, for meditation and stimulation, is mainly about the personal side of things: my and your day-to-day relation with Jesus Christ. This book loosely follows the pattern yet, by accident more than design, it seems to say more than is usual about the corporate and liturgical aspect. Perhaps its provenance in public addresses is responsible.

It is here that Anglicanism faces a dilemma: it places great stress on corporate worship yet, while vaguely exhorting the faithful to personal devotion, it offers little practical guidance about how to go about it. Lately the emphasis has been reversed; techniques of meditative and contemplative prayer – 'spirituality' – are all the rage, and while there is equal stress on liturgical studies and experiment there is a singular lack of positive instruction on practical participation. The rightly acclaimed movement towards lay-participation should mean more than reading lessons and offering intercession, and more also than the acquisition of liturgical knowledge. What are the devotional and psychological attitudes required to transform a heterogeneous congregation into the organic Body of Christ? And how is the personal–corporate balance actually achieved?

The typical Anglican penchant for exaggerated intellectualism exhorts the faithful to follow the service in a book in order to understand what it means. It is no uncommon sight to see devout and informed Anglicans burying their noses in the book during the elevation of the sacred host: hang on a bit Jesus, while I brush up my Christology and have another little think about the real presence; then I can pay attention to you, if there is time. In what mood do we enter into it all, what is our attitude, our motives, our self-giving and thankful reception of grace outpoured? Can we transcend the intellectual?

To sum up in two ghastly expressions, to be a 'practising Christian' means 'going to church'. Agreed that you cannot have one without the other – if either phrase actually means anything – but let us try to do a bit better. Perhaps the cathedral's Girl in the Bikini, in chapter 5, has something to teach us? Possibly she may offer another good reason for our chosen idiom, for it overrules that notorious Anglican tension, or pseudo-respectability, which frustrates genuine worship through embracing either puritanical joylessness on the one hand or pious sentimentality on the other.

The bulk of the book is concerned with analogy, lightsomely with parable, which, based upon the Thomist theory of *analogia entis* – analogy of being – is a necessary process for thinking or speaking about divine mystery. But its limitations must be understood and accepted, for no human language is adequate to speak directly about God. To call God 'Father' can only mean that his relation with us is *something like* human paternity, but it is never quite the same. It follows that analogy never proves anything, it cannot issue in dogmatic truth, there is always a snag, a deficiency; yet for illumination, for spiritual insight and illustration it can, guided by the Spirit, lead to perception beyond the rational.

It is after all our Lord's own method, he spoke in parables, purposely enlightening to some and not to others. So analogy becomes a necessary risk, especially when we descend from the sublimity of the New Testament to my home-spun variety. I hope some of these might be enlightening: but be warned!

2

A Fruitful Fast

The ninth chapter of St Mark's Gospel tells the story of the disciples' abortive attempt to heal the boy with a dumb spirit. Jesus did not mince words: 'O faithless generation, how long shall I be with you? how long shall I suffer you? bring him unto me.' The disciples failed through lack of faith: 'This kind can come forth by nothing but by prayer.' Scholars tell us that a later scribe, strong in piety if not too conscientious over sub-editing etiquette, added 'and fasting'.

The story takes us to the heart of lenten aspiration by suggesting a synthesis of three elements – faith, prayer, fasting – conjoined in that order and forming a pattern of redemptive creativity. Notice that it was the disciples as a body who failed, with neither failure nor faithlessness imputed to any single one of them. So it is with the power of the Church with which we are concerned, with the corporate church local, with the Christian body to which we belong, and not primarily with our own comfort, prayer or progress; not even with our own moral struggle, although these personal aspects all come in some-where. In second place in fact.

The story puts strong emphasis on cosmic evil, the boy suffered more than physical dumbness – the disciples might have dealt with that – he suffered also diabolical possession. Now as then, our real battle is against spiritual wickedness in the heavenly realm. Can such a mission be light-hearted? There is a sense in which it cannot be anything else, for it is too serious, too stupendous a reality, too great a mystery, to be understood in our finitude.

So we have to return to the personal and local, to put up our little fight for faith, to deepen our poor devotion, but in the certain hope that it is part of the cosmic redemption of the whole universe in Christ. Our efforts become petty unless and until we regain this ultimate perspective, until we see the vision, however dimly, of the redemption of the world by our Lord Jesus Christ, the means of grace and the hope of glory. In this perspective we may now get on with our lenten exercises.

Only faith can remove the mountains of evil, suffering and despair, yet 'this kind goeth not out but by prayer'. So Lent is about prayer, in all of its aspects and sub-divisions: personal, liturgical, meditative, contemplative, joyous and penitential. The not-too-grimly-serious approach to prayer – our eternal, baptismal relation with God in Christ – without tension, artificiality, or mock piety, is that which helps to deepen our faith. Only false pride in our own spiritual capacity destroys it: 'Lord I believe, help thou mine unbelief.'

The scribe who played around with St Mark's original text, adding 'and fasting' by his own personal whim, has in the end done us a good turn. He has got things in perspective and the right way round; Lent means faith, to be deepened and expanded, then prayer, since this is how it so happens, with fasting as subsidiary support. Fasting I take to mean all those disciplines – mental, psychological, practical and physical – which are supportive of prayer. A common error is to divorce the two and reverse their order. We all have a potential for the unleashing of spiritual power through a local community, but such potential, given in baptism and sustained by grace, is uncreative until it is harnessed, bridled, broken and trained. This potential is as the strength of a wild horse, power without discipline, but the most rigorous rule of fasting is like harness without a horse; the brazen bits may look quaint hanging on the wall, but they are not of much use. So whatever our lenten rule of fasting may be it has to be subjected to two constant questions: Does this in any way help and support prayer? Then, Is this deepening faith to the destruction of evil, first in me, then in my community, then cosmically? It matters little how small our efforts appear, so long as we maintain the transcendental, cosmic perspective.

St Paul introduced the analogy of the spiritual athlete to the church in Corinth: 'I therefore so run, not as uncertainly; so fight I not as one that beateth the air.' The boxer trains, fasts, undergoes intensive discipline, not least of the mind, for the one purpose of beating his opponent. It would be folly to go through all that training if there was to be no fight at the end; folly to accept self-denial with no serious prayer to be supported by it. St Paul elaborates his analogy: the ordinary athlete does all this to win a temporal, soon to be forgotten honour; the spiritual athlete is concerned with the eternal dimension.

To switch the analogy, perhaps it is a little like active membership in a political party. There is a sense in which the result of a general election is too big an issue for little me to exert much influence on; what does even my vote really matter? For I have never known of a member of parliament to have been elected by a majority of one. Yet we all know that my vote does matter when it is placed in the wider context of local party organization. If the party wins we have a real share in the victory, even if our candidate has a majority of ten thousand. So the local Christian can give much to the local Christian organism, then to the spiritual power of the universal Church in its fight against cosmic evil. If we, or I, miss out on the lenten discipline, does it really matter? In our local churches is there really any difference between 148 communicants and 147? Can my little contribution, my little fasts and spiritual struggles, add anything of significance to the cosmic battle against the diabolical? Lord help thou mine unbelief, for if we are truly in Christ, truly incorporated into the sacred humanity, the answer to these questions must be 'Yes'.

In any seemingly benevolent act of divine providence, in any part of the world, individual Christians may believe that they have played a part. Regrettably the converse is also true; we all bear personal responsibility for all evil everywhere. Our Lent is a paradox: our small fasts, our fragile attempts at prayer, any attempt to strengthen our feeble faith in the local Christian community is nevertheless part of an extension of the victory of the cross.

Finally, we should widen our vision, accepting the paradoxical relation between the seemingly trivial and the eternal, between the everyday simplicity of devotion and its cosmic significance. So to the practicalities of lenten rule.

Because of the foregoing the conventional little lenten fasts – no sugar, confectionery, tobacco, alcohol – are not to be despised. Self-denial for the love of God can be prayerful, stimulating and recollective, but the motive is all important, especially in the face of a double distortion which has recently crept in. The motive for the love of God is replaced by almost its reverse; fasting for personal well-being. Discard sugar, cream buns and afternoon tea and the food fanatics will be at you before you can say avoirdupois; yes, you are a bit overweight, how sensible to fast a bit, it will be so good for you. Give up your pipe and the cancer scare recedes; forego your gin and tonic and no more worries about the breathalyser. All too true, but it makes a farce of a recollective Lent: for the love of God. As the lenten collect has it, Jesus' forty days in the wilderness was 'for our sakes'.

The second distortion is that for thousands who have virtually given up any serious attempt at the life of faith, it degenerates into folk-religion, like pancake day without the shriving and Christmas Mass at midnight for goodness knows why. Self-denial for the love of God, however seemingly trivial, may take on the character of our Lord's forty days, as preparation for the fight against sin, which is still part of the vicarious principle and which, within the sacred humanity, has eternal significance.

But there are more obviously creative fasts, foremost of which is that which provides the necessary *time* for a lenten concentration of formal prayer. We are reminded again of St Paul's boxing analogy in 1 Corinthians 9. The boxer must keep himself in trim all year round, the Christian has to maintain his day-to-day relationship with Christ all year round, yet in both cases there is a concentrated period – again in both cases possibly six weeks or forty days plus contemplative Sundays – in immediate preparation for the big fight. That is how Jesus did it in the wilderness, forty days of training then the fight, the temptation, and the knock-out blow: 'Get thee hence Satan – 8 – 9 – 10 – out.' We too can beat Satan in the confessional ring – it should have been yesterday, shriving Tuesday, but it is never too late. *Te absolvo* says the referee: 8 – 9 – 10 – *out*.

On the simplest level one can give up a favourite radio programme, or the weekly journal, or an extra half-hour in bed, in order to make time for prayer. But there is a particularly modern aspect of this principle. For all sorts of subtle reasons, spiritual, psychological and sociological, modern Christians are moving away from discursive meditation towards simple contemplative prayer. It is part of the existential stance which, like it or not, we are all engulfed in. It is part of the contemporary cultural pattern. Briefly and as simply as possible it is a movement from intellectualism to living experience, from substantive thought – What is it made of? What does it mean? – to the empirical – What does it feel like? From academic concern with the attributes of God to our personal experience of his presence.

It is possible to make a discursive meditation on a biblical narrative in twenty minutes, simple contemplative prayer takes longer. So what about two or three hours of quiet in the presence of God every lenten Saturday afternoon instead of an extra twenty minutes on the other six days? What, no football? What, no golf? Or perhaps Sunday? The traditional day of restful contemplation – for in biblical context the rest for the people of God and the contemplation of God mean much the same thing – set aside for the sublime creative art of doing nothing in the divine presence? What, no *News of the World*? Most of us would do well to emulate Chesterton's Father Brown: 'There was no man who had a more hearty and enduring appetite for doing nothing' (*The Green Man*).

It is the Protestant ethic that teaches that the Devil will find work for idle hands to do, which is a subtle off-shoot of the musty old heresy called Pelagianism, and an even more diabolical subtlety as it contradicts the real Protestant foundation of justification by faith alone. A more orthodox interpretation would be that, as E. L. Mascall points out, it is the devil's work which is always manifested in useless activity. Who 'as a roaring lion, walketh about, seeking whom he may devour . . .' He does not need to devour anything because he is not hungry; he just cannot keep still, and I suspect that we can get Satan into something of a diabolical panic if we show him that we can keep still. 'Whom resist steadfast in the faith;' the stand-up fight has to come in the end, but it was Jesus' forty days of silent preparation that got Satan bewildered and groggy in the first place.

'If at first you don't succeed try, try, and try again.' Well yes, there is something to be said for courageous persistence, but if at first, or second, or third, you don't succeed, how about giving up for a bit? I can't, Jesus, you take over. We have all suffered from abortive ambition, we have tried and tried and failed: what a relief to give in, to yield to Christ, in the silent wilderness!

In biblical typology the wilderness stands for contemplative silence. This was Jesus' wilderness technique; his training for the coming conflict was the maintenance of a perfect contemplative unity with the Father. Essential to all rules of religious Orders are periods of such silence. According to circumstances, could not this be transferred to the domestic sphere, as it was at Little Gidding? Anglican spirituality strangles itself with words, the lauded glories of the Book of Common Prayer are all very well, yet it can become impossibly verbose. Periods of silence undertaken by a mature Christian household would be a wonderful Christian discipline: give up *words* for Lent.

Compare Jesus' wilderness experience with that of Elijah in 1 Kings 19. Jesus achieved harmony with the Father throughout, and also with the wild beasts, so that he was united with the universe, winning the victory vicariously, on behalf of the whole. Christ fled *to* the Father, Elijah fled *from* Jezebel, and found things much more complicated. 'What are you doing here, Elijah?' The answer should have been 'Nothing' but Elijah had to justify himself in terms of activity. 'I have been very jealous for the Lord, the God of hosts . . .' 'What are you doing here, Elijah?' Same answer: it took him a long time to get the message. Earthquakes, fires and hurricanes are such noisy things which have to be silenced before the divine voice is heard.

Lenten discipline is not for seeking the Lord, but for adopting the position where he can find us, in silence and solitude, in patient waiting not hectic activity. Little Zacchaeus had the right idea (Luke 19). He could not reach the Lord for the crowds and the noise and his littleness of stature, so he climbed up a tree and waited in solitude and silence.

3

The Thomist Football League

For the sake of the uninitiated let me explain the ramifications of the English football league. For any possible transatlantic reader it should not be too difficult to translate the analogy into the American game (this might be more difficult when we get on to cricket in chapter 6).

The league comprises ninety-two clubs divided into four divisions. The first division consists of the best, the top grade, and the most wealthy, with magnificent grounds and stadia. The second division is roughly the same but not quite, and we shall see the significance of this later. It is also important to see that there are subtle variations within these two divisions themselves, as well as something of an overlap. For example the few clubs at the top of the first division are considerably superior to those at the bottom, and yet the top team in the second division may be as good as or better than the bottom club in the first division.

There is a considerable gap between the second and third divisions, the latter being plainly inferior, in play, status and dignity. And the fourth division is pretty rough stuff, with far less skill and technique. The analogy will not be complete until we bring in a knock-out competition – the Football Association Cup – in which all the clubs take part, as well as others who are not in the professional league at all. The Cup is especially exciting because it gives the inferior clubs a chance to play against the cream of the first division, often with surprising results.

St Thomas Aquinas explained God's creation as a hierarchy of being. At the bottom of the scale, or league, the fourth division, is the world of inanimate matter, rocks, water, bits of dead wood and so on. Next up the scale is the living world as we know it, plants and trees, insects, reptiles, fish, birds and animals, all headed by the special sort of mammal *homo sapiens*. Then comes the unseen sphere of the spirit inhabited by the saints perfected in glory; or in theological terms the Church

Triumphant. At the peak of the hierarchy is what is traditionally called heaven inhabited by a further hierarchy of created beings: 'therefore with angels and archangels and all the company of heaven we laud and magnify thy Holy Name'. In past ages speculative and gnostic theology went to town on all this: seraphim, cherubim, thrones, dominations, powers, principalities, before we get down to angels and archangels. It is all treated in mystical speculation in the *Divine Comedy* of Dante, but the important thing here is to recognize at least the probability that the heavenly sphere – the hierarchical first division – is the most complex aspect of the whole creation.

We are apt to think of heaven, if we consider it at all, as a sort of monochrome sphere of cloud and shadow. C. S. Lewis said that heaven must contain more colour not less than our world, more not less complexity of harmony than you can wring out of a piano keyboard, and if you happen to bump into an angel, rather than gliding through a phantom you are likely to bounce off with considerable force. Heaven and its inhabitants are more real not less than anything we know of in the present life.

The first point in translating the analogy, which can come as a surprise to many a devout Christian and a traumatic shock to the humanists, is that *homo sapiens* finds his rightful place in the divine economy as head of the third division, and nowhere near the bottom of the first, with promotion to the second division as his greatest hope and ultimate goal. Although the league itself is a unity, and the Thomist hierarchy of being is one divine creation, humankind is eternally barred from division one; we might share in the perfected glory of the angels but we shall never be one. All we can hope for, and all we should and need to hope for is a lowly position in the Church Triumphant, the sphere of the saints in division two.

A great deal of mischief is done by bandying about the unbiblical notion that man is 'lord of creation'. If he is lord of anything it is as top of the third division, and if we look around the contemporary scene and ask precisely who or what power controls our civilization, even this modest status looks doubtful. God created heaven and earth and put men and women in charge of the earthy part. God created the animals and instructed Adam to name them, that is to give them status and dignity. As the deeply theological Ladybird series of nursery rhymes has it:

> The animals went by one by one,
> And Adam said this sure is fun,
> Now what is that? I wish I knew –
> But I rather think it's a kangaroo.

We are in the third division of the total league, we have our ordained place in the whole hierarchy of creation, so we must now consider in more detail our relation with the other three divisions, for it is only this total dimension that tends towards a healthy spirituality: only this perspective makes sense of giving up sugar for Lent. First we must look to our relation with all the other aspects of our own division three, for a spiritual harmony here and from here to the rest of the created universe is the foundation for contemplative prayer.

If we are in any sense lord of this little created planet, it must be benevolent lordship not despotic tyranny; we are not supreme rulers but rather ambassadors of Christ, our planet's ultimate redeemer as well as creator. Somewhat old-fashioned theology used to speak of an interdependence between all things in a natural order; the old argument from design, and this way of thinking retains a value. It has been pointed out that the so-called lord of the earth, of this planet, is nevertheless dependent on it at every point. In *Christian Universe* E. L. Mascall reminds us that we cannot keep alive on the merely physical level without absorbing bits of animals and plants into our stomachs.

More pertinently a spiritual harmony, a rapport, with our environment is sometimes called the first form of contemplation, and Mascall tells us in the same book that we are unlikely to achieve a loving relationship with each other or with society at large until we have achieved harmony with the material environment. A country walk between lovers is not going to come off if one loves the rural scene and the other hates it. This brings us back to the need, in Lent or at any other time, for the quest of solitude and silence; for the spiritual efficacy of doing nothing for Lent; of watching the snowdrops instead of the telly.

All of which leads naturally into our relation with the fourth division, with the world of inanimate matter. Let us first bring to mind that it is, by biblical affirmation, very good. Rocks and stones, minerals and metals are all very good and redeemable, made glorious, by human creativity inspired by grace. As Evelyn Underhill taught, chunks of stone and lumps of iron can be contemplative mandala: Hugh of St Victor and St Francis of Assisi said much the same thing. But the same goes for a lighted candle or a flaming lump of coal, and the same even more for cathedrals, iron bridges and steel pylons. What of finding time to take such things with contemplative seriousness – for Lent.

Having been a philistine farmer early in life I have always been, and remain, suspicious of aesthetic sentimentality about nature. I still hold that the best thing to do with a moorland wilderness is to plough it up and redeem it; be that as it may, inanimate matter, the fourth division, is to be loved and respected. It can be argued that we need some bits of wilderness for contemplative purposes, although I still prefer the Fens to Dartmoor as inspiration for prayer. In short, never despise the fourth division.

So in heart and mind we ascend to the second division, hoping to ascend there more fully after this earthly sojourn. In more usual terminology, we ascend from the Church Militant to the Church Expectant, thence to the Church Triumphant in heaven. So Lent, or Christian life at any time, must be incomplete without a prayerful interpretation of the doctrine of the Communion of Saints. The most important thing about the saints is that they are alive, and it follows that they are contemporaries. We arrive at the traditional lenten exercise of spiritual reading; but what and how to read?

The diversity of tone, approach and idiom in the writings of the saints is inexhaustible; they are all different, and yet this mass of devotional writing is roughly classifiable into types or schools. Every Christian, by *attrait*, outlook or temperament also fits, again roughly, into one or other of these schools. There is nothing to worry about if certain writings, however famous, fail to satisfy, or seem even repulsive. The immediate job is to discover which of the saints or saintly schools make an immediate appeal. Many a devout Christian will have discovered this already, for those who have not there are two courses open: first to experiment, to pick up many of the classic works and so browse through them until one strikes an immediate chord. Such experiment would itself constitute a valuable lenten exercise which would lay a good foundation for the future. Do not take a book at random with a conscientious proviso that you must go through with it; if it does not fit get rid of it and have a taste of something else.

A second and possibly better way is to seek advice, since the whole process, which could take some time, under the guidance of a competent spiritual director, will also lay a firm foundation for the future.

Having made the discovery read as though from a contemporary; read St Bernard, or St Augustine, or Jeremy Taylor, or anyone else as if it were this month's issue of a religious journal, as if the author was alive – which he is – and writing personally to you. There may be differences in style and idiom, the most modern writer can still be out-of-date, and fashions change, but the central messages of the saints are of eternal significance.

As our contemporaries, the saints also have personal relations with us as individuals. The concept of saintly patronage is no mere sentiment, as a live and contemporary St John has a real and special relation with St John's parish, St John's college, and John Smith: Holy Martin *ora pro nobis*. Of course you might not get on too well with the writings of your patron saint, the boss can always be awkward, but find out who you do get on with and the patron-boss will not mind. It is accepted as natural and sensible for the Franciscans to be devoted to St Francis, the Benedictines to St Benedict, and the Cistercians to St Bernard; personal patronage is only an extension of the same principle.

There are many who, while easily accepting, and acting upon the doctrine of the Communion of Saints, find more difficulty in working out their relation with the first division. But the whole hierarchy of heaven are also our living contemporaries: we say so at every celebration of the Eucharist. And the whole hierarchy of heaven cannot be less than personal, the arch-angels are even known by personal names: Michael, Gabriel and Raphael. It is all part of the celestial ladder which leads to God, the ladder which begins with chunks of rock as manifestation of the divine, and ends with the worship given by seraphim and cherubim in which we take part. The overriding truth behind St Thomas and the football league is that this illustrates what is the real world in which we live, and if the four divisions constitute one league there is perpetual interplay between them.

Here is the significance of the Football Association Cup, which is played out alongside the league matches but in which the clubs all get mixed up; first division versus third or fourth, second division against third. In the Cup matches the little fourth-division club, with a modest ground surrounded by a few wooden seats and an average spectatorship of a few hundred gets the chance of a match with a first-division team, before sixty thousand people cheering from opulent grandstands all around the ground. We humans of the third division come right up against the saints of the second, and may hopefully get an occasional glimpse of the hierarchy in heaven.

We have been unashamedly speaking in spatial terms, following ancient, patristic or scholastic usage and based on biblical cosmology: the three-tier universe. In such language the Church Militant is here on earth, the Church Expectant in paradise is 'above', and the Church Triumphant in heaven is further 'above' that; heaven is the firmament 'on high' from which the incarnate Lord 'descends'. There is still no reason why we should not think in this way, so long as we recognize it as analogical, symbolic and illustrative. Thus we think of the Church as a three-storey building with a basement underlying the first and second floors. The Eucharist is sometimes seen as a lift, celebrated in the earthly basement yet linking it with the next two floors; all the saints are present at every celebration which is offered in the Holy Spirit, through the Son, to God the Father almighty, and it is offered 'with angels and archangels and all the company of heaven'.

Despite the outmoded, in fact bluntly erroneous cosmology, there is nothing wrong with this so long as we accept biblical typology and realize exactly what we are doing. But the Thomist football league has the advantage of being rid of this way of thinking. In all cases the Church is one, the universe is one, an organic unity, and so is the football league; they do not need ladders or lifts to join up the forms or storeys or divisions. All the clubs play at the same time and on the same level. In this analogy the Eucharist is not a lift but a horizontal channel. The ninety-two clubs are separated as modes or spheres of activity but not necessarily spacially: intersecting circles form a better diagram than three floors arranged vertically. In other words heaven and earth, men and saints are contemporary in activity and conjoined in existence. The spacial–vertical design is legitimate but unnecessary; devotionally we are nearer to the saints and nearer to the angels, separate but on the same universal plane. One does not need a lift to carry the saints down to the altar, they are there already and all the time, so are the angels. Neither do you need a lift from which Jesus descends from 'heaven'; the Eucharist is a manifestation of his Presence rather than a vehicle that arranges it. The Eucharist does not create the grace of God through Christ but makes it available, usable, efficacious.

It is also in the Eucharist that proper prominence is given to the significance of the fourth division, the realm of inanimate matter, for the Eucharist is usually celebrated on an altar which is traditionally and correctly constructed of stone. It is celebrated in a consecrated place which is also made of stone, while its necessary equipment is chalice and paten formed out of precious metal, rightly ornamented with precious stones: perhaps there is mystical significance in the masses of jewels mentioned in St John's apocalypse? Then there is bread and wine consecrated by a Christian community, all from the third division, while we have seen how the two higher divisions, saints and angels are ever present. All these together, as a whole, stress the sanctification and final redemption of the whole universe, but here in the Eucharist we do not need lifts and storeys to unify that universe; all is temporal and all is eternal.

It is hoped that this analogy, this parable, might help a little to widen the scope of eucharistic worship. Many of the faithful think in terms of hearing the Word, worshipping the blessed Trinity, partaking of the fruits of our Lord's passion, of receiving life-giving, cleansing grace; all of which is right and good, but the analogy of the Thomist universe tends to further enrichment, it widens the vision and brings in the transcendental element.

If analogical thinking has its inherent dangers, it also

provides safeguards against error and distortion. As already noted, it guards against immanentalism, and keeps alive eucharistic enthusiasm in our duller periods of aridity. It also opposes Pelagianism, which is the bastard child of pride, because it deepens faith by extending its boundaries. Our analogy here quite literally 'puts us in our place'; top of division three not of division one. These two aspects properly combine the Church universal with the church local. It is right to stress the power of the local community, to intercede for those in need within that community, but against a cosmic background this is brought into proportion. By all means offer prayer for friends and neighbours, for Jack in hospital and Jill in distress; intercede also for the tragedies of the wider world. Yet keep to the perspective which assures that the offering of the Eucharist itself is sufficient intercession for everything there is to intercede for: it pierces all the divisions 'with angels and archangels'.

A further all-important safeguard is against the prevalent heresy which theology calls angelism: the desire to be an angel, to be done with the ridiculous human body, to jump straight into division one, without effort or training. With the deepest humility we honour the faith and courage of the handicapped, the patience of the distressed and seriously sick, but the temptation is strong to grumble at God for making us human, for placing us in the third division, especially when things go wrong. In our prime of life we rightly thank God for all the blessings of this life, for food and drink, sex and love, but how we detest the body when it hurts. St Francis had the humility to call it brother ass, acceptable under God's providential order. With a little application the analogy helps to redeem our suffering, to share it with Christ who, infinitely above and beyond all the divisions in the whole league, deigned to play in division three and there to suffer unimaginable tortures. The Word became flesh; he did not take the short cut of becoming an angel.

How then can we make our worship more real? How do we enter into the Eucharist? Not by going to church as spectators but by going home, to our Father's house where we belong. Above all by recognizing that our little local family of God is of cosmic significance in all it does. Let us breach the temporal while living in time, for it is only by the abject humility that goes with division three that we can truly see how important we are. Let us enter the eucharistic throng to receive what we cannot do without, then to give, and ultimately to give in.

4

The Woodlouse Sermon

I am very fond of woodlice: *isopoda armadillidiidae*. All the best cathedral sermons have a bit of superfluous Latin, it raises the tone of the thing and makes everyone feel learned, although curiously enough we shall see that this bit of latinity is not wholly irrelevant.

They are catholic little creatures because their habitat is universal, they are found under various sub-species in pretty well every country in the world. Many such foreign species have somehow got themselves imported into this country and have established themselves in company with the native British variety, which conversely have managed to get themselves established in most other countries: quite Anglican in fact.

So I feel some friendly rapport with the woodlouse, and was considerably upset one winter morning when I collected the last of my heap of logs, exposing a startled colony of them. They behaved characteristically; some attempted a flight to the wilderness, and I so much hope that many reached it. Others formed themselves into close little communities for what protection they could find, I tried to help them find a more suitable abode but regrettably without much success. There were others who rolled themselves up into little balls, as is their wont, for protection against predators, yet seemingly accepting martyrdom with uncomplaining fortitude.

How different was their response to that of an anthill under similar circumstances; a disturbed anthill degenerates into a solid mass of feverish activity which gets the ants nowhere. Ants are not only essentially Pelagian, but also exponents of the coarser aspects of the Protestant ethic: work hard for material success and the Lord will reward you. Disturb other creatures, like hares, and they will rush off all alone, proudly rejecting assistance from any quarter. Ants have to be in community, the wrong sort of little communists, loyal to the system but utterly incapable of personal initiative: an ant never comes up with an original idea. Hares are loners, not because they are of unique genius but because they are incapable of creative relationship: then comes March and they go mad.

But woodlice have got it all: community interplay, creative dialogue, yet always capable of going in search of the wilderness, of running a risk and taking a chance; even to the extent of rolling themselves up in little balls, hoping for the best and willing to cope with the worst. They have the supreme gift of being able to give in.

So the last log disturbed me as well as them. It was so cold, and I would willingly have given up my lovely wood fire if that would have meant happiness and satisfaction for a single woodlouse. But the damage having been done, simply replacing the last log would have achieved nothing. So what could I do to put things right? I could see answers to the problem; a few feet away there was a big stone slab, suitably damp and dank, probably a better place than the original log. I could lift it and shoo the woodlice under it, but they would not be shooed. Force was of no use, for even a rubber spatula would be too rough to avoid damaging them. So I gave up. Then horror of horrors; sitting morosely by the fire a woodlouse emerged from a smouldering crevice. I tried to rescue it from the flames but again without success. The tragedy was that it could easily have saved itself by taking a certain direction, along the log and down a piece of kindling wood that had not yet caught fire; first left and there was the safety of the hearth. This woodlouse would not have been happy on the warm stone, they like damp cold and dark places, but at least this one would have been safe.

What can I do to help them over circumstances in which they cannot help themselves? I have tried talking to them but they cannot understand; I have tried gently, ever so gently, to prod them into a happier environment, but all to no avail. I *am* fond of woodlice, I have even supplied them with very young luscious seedlings which they like to eat, but they still seem to prefer to go their own way in their own good time. Yes I *am* fond of them, but they offer little response; perhaps I am giving way to sentimentality? Perhaps after all they are not worth all the trouble? Let them stew in their own juice. But no, I cannot but be concerned, how *can* I show my love for them?

It is an utterly fantastic idea, but suppose I could somehow manage to enter into direct communication with them? Could I pretend to *be* a woodlouse? In fact could I actually become a woodlouse? Then I could talk to them in their own language, demonstrate a better way, but what would that entail? Could I, or would I, give up my humanity, forego for ever perhaps the joys of human culture, no more art, music or literature? No more robust physical pleasures like eating partridge and drinking claret, no more family life with a humanly loving wife and family, for woodlice are hermaphrodite. All this sacrifice in an analogical way is roughly what theology means by *kenosis*; a total self-emptying on behalf of an infinitely inferior species. Do I really love woodlice as much as that? Would I freely make such a sacrifice on their behalf? In the famous words of Eliza Doolittle: 'not bloody likely'. Not least because I have a hunch that, with all the goodwill in the world, the experiment would turn out to be bloody. Yes, woodlice are charming little creatures, clean and wholesome, doing harm to nobody and nothing, but I doubt if they would accept me. I doubt if they would understand my good intentions, and I doubt if they would really understand objective love. There would be every chance that they would reject my advice and object to my interference; they would turn on me and push me into an heretical ant-hill, to be torn apart and crucified.

The analogy hardly needs translation, except to add that to turn me into a woodlouse is an infinitely small step compared with turning God into man. For, returning to St Thomas Aquinas, humans and woodlice are on the same strata in the hierarchy of creation, we are both in the third division of the league, while God is creator of the total league, infinitely above and beyond the universe. Let us maintain at all costs the transcendental element, and yet there is the corresponding immanental side of things.

There are scores of analogies which attempt, never with complete success, to explain the doctrine of the one, holy and undivided Trinity, and there are all sorts of devotional techniques which attempt to give mystical insight into what is beyond the rational, like the contemplation of the clover leaf with three lobes, or a triangle, or intersecting circles, or the star of David. There is a tiny country church in Cornwall in which the roof of the sanctuary is decorated with sixteen different signs or *mandala* of the holy Trinity, the contemplation of any of which may give deeper insight into this intimate mystery than tome upon tome of academic reasoning. Not that such studies are superfluous; discursive consideration of the first portion of the *Quicunque Vult*, the so-called Athanasian creed, is a good, even essential prolegomena to the contemplation of *mandala*.

Could further symbolism add anything to our understanding? Perhaps, perhaps not. I sincerely hope that the following will not prove offensive to any reader; it might even be deemed impious, of going too far, but I take the risk. What trinitarian pattern emerges from the contemplation of a woodlouse?

As with the Athanasian creed, or similar formula, we have to begin with a few doctrinal facts, which is where our cathedral sermon custom of using a bit of Latin comes into its own. Biologically speaking a woodlouse, *isopoda armadillidiidae* looks as if it has a family resemblance with a beetle, or a centipede or some similar creature, but no. The woodlouse is not *coleopterous* or *cheilopoda* but *isopoda*, and its nearest relation, believe it or not, is a lobster. A further characteristic of a woodlouse is that its bodily waste products are converted into ammonia and exhaled as a gas through its whole body. What is called sulphate of ammonia in agriculture is a basic nitrogenous fertilizer supplying the most elemental and essential plant nutrient, so the gaseous exhalation from the woodlouse into the atmosphere unleashes nitrogen which sustains the vegetable kingdom and maintains soil fertility upon which all earthly life depends. Woodlice exhale life-giving properties. Dig up a broad bean plant and you will probably find two things: nodules that smell of ammonia and woodlice. Beans, peas, clover and all *leguminosae* share this characteristic with woodlice: they both *give* life-giving nutrient to soil and atmosphere rather than absorbing it for their own self-centred purposes.

So where is our analogy now? C. S. Lewis was accused of impiety or worse by looking through the eyes of Screwtape and seeing God as the Enemy. Yet the blessed Trinity is often described in terms of cold unfeeling geometry: triangles and leaves of clover and so on. Is it going too far, with due recognition of all the pitfalls of analogical reasoning, to think of God-the-Father-Lobster, the woodlouse Incarnate, and the all-pervading, immanent, life-giving Spirit of Ammonia-Nitrogenous gas which – or rather who – proceeds from them? After all the Lobster and the Woodlouse are of one substance – *isopoda* – and in this context we need not get all that stewed up about the *filioque* clause.

If I am not blowing my own trumpet too loudly there must be something in an analogy which schoolgirls, listening to a cathedral sermon by compulsion rather than choice, can remember after several years. How they interpret it is another question, yet we are taught to believe in the ultimate re- demption, the christification (in Teilhard de Chardin's terminology) of all created things. It is possible that some are led to affective devotion of Jesus in his passion when they see a woodlouse caught in the flames; they might even think of the all-pervading Spirit when they see woodlice and broad beans giving off life-giving, sanctifying nitrogen.

It might prove to be a little more memorable, a bit more exciting, than triangles and clover leaves. And what is wrong in recollecting the love of our heavenly Father while we enjoy a lightsome lobster on Fridays in Lent?

5

The Girl in the Bikini

After a year of service in an English cathedral, especially one in a popular tourist area like Cornwall, one of the most striking impressions is the difference between winter and summer. Worship in winter is concentrated on a regular congregation of faithful residents, a compact, close-knit expression of the Body of Christ. It is all rather staid and sedate, but certainly not gloomy. Liturgy tends to become a little tense and regimented, and for some reason or other everyone seems to be dressed in dark clothes. It is all very respectable, even C. of E. inhibited.

There is a healthier side. Autumnal gloom and winter darkness lends an atmosphere of mystery, of numinous wonder; darkness, like silence, can be a wonderful stimulus to prayer. And a Gothic building of cathedral proportions seems always to display its places of contemplative twilight, even on a sunny day. There is a particular difference between an early celebration of the Eucharist in winter, when it is foggy outside and the chapel appears as a holy oasis of divine light within almost sinister gloom all around, and the same celebration with sun pouring through coloured glass, showing up saints and symbols.

Although there can be no theological difference, cathedral evensong in winter, with the choir picked out as by a spotlight and a congregation of half a dozen lurking in a dusky nave, seemingly acres of it, is a spiritual exercise in its own right. The essentially vicarious aspect of the divine office, its objectivity, its conjunction with the worship of saints and angels and all the company of heaven, is forceably brought out. The same thing on a summer Sunday, is, curiously, not quite the same thing. The emphasis changes from the eternal worship of the Church Triumphant to the temporal expression of that offering by the Church Militant here on earth.

In summer, in the height of the tourist season, a huge change takes place. The church local, the close-knit family of God, is happily still there, in the centre of things, otherwise even the

Eucharist would appear to degenerate into a sacred concert or even that liturgical abomination we call a 'special service'. But now this resident hard core of the faithful is surrounded by, supported by, large numbers of happy holiday-makers, the majority of whom are regular attenders at their home parish churches. It is quite erroneous to assume, over optimistically, that the cathedral has the capacity of attracting vast numbers of the uncommitted just because they happen to be on vacation. And of course such a congregation is made up of Anglicans, and possibly others, of many traditions and shades of church-manship.

The result is a curious mixture of attitudes. On the one hand a different sort of unholy tension arises, people are not too sure as to what will happen next, just a trifle ill at ease. For being mostly Anglicans they are brainwashed into believing that liturgy means that everybody has to do exactly the same thing at exactly the same time as everybody else. If we are not careful the heavenly banquet becomes a canteen meal at a second-rate conference centre. The happy family of God takes on the horrible characteristic of a military parade ground. As Dom Cuthbert explained the domestic ethos of Benedictinism, a regiment is drilled, a family is not.

On the other hand how grateful we are for the brave spirits on holiday who relieve the tension by taking their devotion with an easy freedom. Some even laugh out loud at my jokes during the sermon – how can I thank them enough! In summer there is also a change of attire. Being Anglicans most of the tourists cannot quite shake off some semblance of English churchy respect-ability, but again the braver spirits turn up in open-neck shirts and linen slacks; the ladies come in flowery cotton frocks, bare-shouldered and stockingless. It is healthily refreshing and devotionally helpful. So we come to the famous, or notorious, occasion.

Consternation in the crypt! Panic in the sacristy! It was a glorious hot day in August with lots of well-behaved, scantily clad children. And the Girl: she arrived in a sort of bright-coloured beach robe, a good ten minutes before the Eucharist was due to start; she prayed devoutly for some time, giving a pronounced impression of proficiency; she knew what she was doing without ostentation or embarrassment (canons learn the knack of distinguishing the devoted lambs from the well-meaning goats). But in the shade of the cathedral the thermometer rose to 95 degrees and the girl sensibly shed her beach robe while even some of the more restrained removed their jackets. Beneath the beach robe was a garment known to the trade I believe as a bikini; a bathing suit of quite remarkably skimpy dimensions.

This was just a little too much for our worthy vergers and lay assistants on duty who, after a hurried conference, decided to consult higher authority as to how to cope with this dire emergency. It is our happy boast that the Dean and Chapter of Truro work together amicably as a happy band of brothers. We manage to agree over most important points of policy, in the end: but we are not renowned for the snap decision. So this emergency caught us on the hop: what was to be done about the girl in the bikini? There were various suggestions: could she be persuaded to replace the beach robe? But it was a thick towelling garment and it was 95 degrees in the shade. Perhaps she could be offered a place in a cooler part of the building where she would be a little less conspicuous: one of the side chapels was quite delightful? Or as a last resort, in the just cause of ecclesiastical decorum, should she be asked to leave? What did the Canon-Chancellor think? ——

This dignitary is what the Middle Ages called *scholasicus*, who passed judgement in heresy trials, and who was expected to be capable of reducing any emergency decision to sound theological principle. Characteristically, on this occasion he was incapable of such constructive thought. Like the Chapter itself the Chancellor was not at his best with snap decisions, and if he had any semblance of theological acumen it was of the kind that took its time.

So in true Anglican, Church of England fashion, we all unanimously decided to do nothing at all. Let her alone and hope for the best.

In the cooler light of Monday morning we thought out the problem more calmly; should we have some formal guide lines that might be applied if such an occasion arose again; what are the principles, if any, of sartorial correctness at public worship? It is a question of some topical significance because, in spite of all the fuss, nonsense and squabble about the vesture of officiating ministers, there is little guidance concerning the laity who all assist: nowadays all the congregation are ministers.

The overriding point is that it occurred to me, on reflection, that the girl in the bikini had a good deal to teach us upon the subject. It could be argued that, taking account of the thousand or so people in the cathedral at that time, including president, assistants, preacher, lectors, servers, choir, and all the rest, it was the girl in the bikini who was dressed most appropriately for the occasion.

Jesus Christ redeemed the universe on the cross, and St Ambrose comments: 'It is important to consider in what condition he ascends the cross; for I see him naked. Let him then who prepares to overcome the world, so ascend that he seek not the appliances of the world . . . He ascends such as nature formed us, God being our creator.' To what extent are our staid dark suits and our shiny shoes 'appliances of the world', feeble attempts to hide ourselves and our sins? I do not know the precise motives behind the bikini – perhaps it was just a hot day – but symbolically at least, how right the girl was. If Christ climbed to the cross, naked and without pretence, wholly self-giving, rejecting even a mild sedation of mulled vinegar, then what is the point of standing proudly upright before that cross clothed with middle-class respectability. The only adequate approach to the risen Redeemer sacramentally present is naked and prostrate.

It will be argued that an audience with the great – queen, patron, prime minister or archbishop – demands some attention to one's appearance. One does not appear unshaven and scruffy because it would be disrespectful, but the analogy fails in the vital point that the Lord of all cannot be placed in the same list as these afore-mentioned worldly personages. There is no doubt that cathedral congregations dress themselves up from the best of motives, yet on the subconscious level it can still be playing a game, depicting a role, subtly pretending to be other than we truly are. The girl in the bikini might also have had mixed motives; there was some discussion as to whether, with the choir in full view, she did not constitute a distraction, or even an occasion of sin, but in symbolic theology she was dead right. We are not told how St Mary Magdalene was dressed at the supper party at Bethany, but I doubt if it was in a black robe and mantilla; in that case how could she have let her hair down? For like the girl in the cathedral that is what she did, both literally and metaphorically; she let her hair down, gave up all pretence, all embarrassment. Here Lord is all I have, the whole honest me, all my worldly appliances, tears and perfume, and above all my love and my sins.

There was once an interminable debate about unworthy reception of Holy Communion, from which there arose the devout custom of making long penitential preparation beforehand. In the days when monthly reception was the norm a whole new series of devotions arose which must have taken the best part of Saturday evening. Finally sacramental confession was enjoined, so that one could communicate worthily. Such a process gives some point to dressing up in one's best clothes on Sunday morning; after all you are absolved, you are worthy, not through personal merit but by Christ's forgiveness.

For the best of reasons and not through laxity this tradition has been superseded by much more frequent communion; the most devout can barely be expected to spend a few hours in penitential preparation two or three times a week. In any case the unworthy reception arguments have more or less died out. Perhaps we have gone too far, but it is the perennial problem of regarding Holy Communion either as the most glorious, wonderful and awesome act there can be, or as a normal part of everyday life that we take in our stride.

But the message of the girl in the bikini, and indeed of St Mary Magdalene, raises a fresh devotional point. Even the corporate absolution within the Eucharist presents a further difficulty. The latter is intended to make us, if not exactly worthy, then at least in a state of grace sufficient for reception of the Lord's Body and Blood. Perhaps we should change into our best clothes immediately after absolution? The ultimate devotional question is what do we actually do with our sins, weaknesses and frailty as we enter the church prior to eucharistic celebration? Do we get rid of them by penitence and absolution, thus leaving them on the doorstep before entering? Or do we approach the altar of God naked, bikini-clad, as we really are, with our sins not left outside but carried in with us? Do we boldly carry all our nasty bits, our shameful, evil, abhorrent, disgusting bits, to the foot of the cross, carrying Jesus in his nakedness, and offer it all to him?

Or do we go on pretending that these bits of us are not really there after all? Or that they are at least happily hidden beneath sartorial respectability?

A problem still arises out of the corporate absolution. It has to be a real absolution, not just a devout liturgical formula, so as we approach the altar there must be a sense in which we *are* cleansed, we *are* worthy communicants. In a curious way it makes things less real, less truly devotional. The liturgical experts will be horrified, but should confession and absolution come *after* communion rather than before? As a glorious consummation instead of a preparation? Should we go to confession in Easter week rather than in Holy Week, for similar reasons?

Or can we somehow square real faith in sacramental absolution with an ability to offer all the nasty bits to Christ as well? Can we accept forgiveness and still be nakedly honest at the altar rail? For, whatever the answer to this conundrum, nakedly honest is what we have to be, all the time and clothes notwithstanding. It is extraordinary what theological speculation, what deep devotional queries, a mini-swimsuit can lead to.

Another liturgical speculation arises, possibly of less importance but nevertheless of some topical interest. There is a vast literature, theology, devotional interpretation about ecclesiastical vesture, and controversy about it all has happily died down. But it might arise in a new form. Such vesture applies only to the ministers of the gospel, from the chasuble of the eucharistic president to the cottas of the choirboys, or even the badges of office of churchwardens. But what happens, in accord with modern pastoral theology, when everyone is a minister? What of the inherent Anglican principle that refuses to drive a wedge between priest and laity? For all are of the Body of Christ; all assist at the Eucharist; the whole Church forms the redemptive organism.

Two things are plain. If there is any value in sacramentalism in its more everyday sense, in symbolism, in a physical manifestation of principle, then go into any Anglican service and it is immediately apparent that minister and congregation are sharply divided by vesture; if we insist that all are theologically one, then it certainly does not look like it. Place the altar in the middle of the building, get rid of the regimented rows of horrid pews, adopt the westward position, go to town on the Pax, and there are still two sorts of people: those dressed up and those not.

The second point is that, to make things rightly consistent, there are simple straight alternatives: either everyone wears a special sort of church vesture, or nobody does. There is something to be said for both solutions.

The latter idea can rightly claim to be the more primitive, a principle beloved by Anglicans, and it is being followed by the equally primitive but revived principle of the house-church. There is still some bewilderment about house-church vesture, and some parish priests would plump for the lot: chasuble, alb, amice, girdle, maniple, stole, even plus biretta if you go in for that sort of thing. Others take the Anglican middle-of-the-road compromise and settle for a cassock. The more adventurous spirits go for anything from a dark suit to flannels and open-neck shirt. So bluntly: If here why not there? If at home why not in church? A few of the most adventurous spirits have faced the question squarely and given up eucharistic vestments altogether and everywhere. We are aware of all the arguments about the presidents representing the Lord, about a chasuble covering, or swamping, the personality of the priest, about a set of high mass vestments emphasizing the corporate solidity of the worshipping church. They are valid arguments pointing to a valid view, but the bikini girl also represents a valid outlook and her message will not go away.

The straight alternative to this viewpoint is for all the congregation to be sure to pick up their wedding garment together with their hymm book as they enter the church. Precisely what shape, colour, pattern or style such should be is open to the wildest speculation, but whatever it was would solve the problem of manifesting a united church at its central rite wherein everyone was a minister and no one a spectator. This may seem far fetched, but it is little different from a uniform tuxedo, and after all we are considering what is correct for a banquet, the wedding breakfast of the bride of Christ. And there is dominical precedent: whatever the shape of the first-century wedding garment, Jesus was pretty tough on the poor chap who had not got one.

If we are to be true to the wider sacramental principle it looks like wedding garments for all or none. Disliking uniform of any kind I go for the latter alternative: the day might come when the whole cathedral congregation turned up with their white collars back to front. That would put paid to a lot of nonsense.

6

Christian Cricket

Apology is necessary to those who do not understand cricket, more especially perhaps to possible readers from across the Atlantic ocean. I much enjoy the great American ball-games, their particular brands of football, ice hockey and basketball. Golf, tennis, swimming and athletics are thoroughly international, while St Paul's *askesis* analogies are confined to running and boxing. Why not use one or other of these less esoteric games as analogy for the organization, function, individual-corporate interplay, and liturgical devotion of the Christian Church? The answer is because, as illumination and insight into all this complicated theology, the cricket analogy is unique and unsurpassed.

There are many other illustrations and metaphors to explain the corporate aspect of the organic Church; the Body of Christ, the Family of God, the Household of Faith. For less biblically based analogies we may think of an orchestra, composed of many players and instruments forged into an harmonious whole. Or of a democratic government, a cabinet, with each member representing a particular department, yet all fitting into a ruling organism. The principle involved is always that membership of the Church, in however humble a capacity, involves active participation and not spectatorship. A congregation is not an audience, nor is it a monochrome assembly line; it consists of woodlice not ants. It is the subtle interaction between unique individuality and corporate organism, between uniquely personal gifts and loyalty: every creature of God is unlike any other, and yet none can survive by itself. If we are not ants neither are we hares.

Reflection indicates that, given these foundation facts, only cricket will do. Any athletic/*askesis* analogy for the Church has to centre on a team game. Incidentally, where St Paul rather falls down is in his individualistic concern with running and boxing, but then he did not know about cricket. He more than makes up for the deficiency with the sublime illustration of the Body of

Christ. But what actually is a team game? It is one with creative interplay between individualism and corporate organism, satisfaction with personal skills and success and the good of the team as a whole.

Many so-called team games veer emphatically to one side or the other. We speak of club or national teams in athletics, swimming, tennis and golf, but these are really questions of individual enterprise, one against one, with a team score added up at the end. On the other hand we speak of individual skills in football or hockey, yet any such individualism is mostly swamped by the total team effort.

Cricket restores both balances. Each member of the team has not only his personal place on the field of play but his own quite specific job; he is batsman or bowler, in-fielder or out-fielder, slip-fielder or wicket-keeper. And the bowlers and batsmen vary in style and technique; slow, fast, off-break, leg-break, righthand, lefthand, top-spin or seamer. Batsmen are openers, middle order, defensive or attacking. Yet the emphasis is still on the team; you can play golf without a team, you can play football with little individuality, but you cannot play cricket without both.

What does all this add up to in the sphere of practical liturgy? Lay-assistance at the Eucharist is more than a selected few being servers, lectors or choir, and it is more than an intelligent following of the service in a wretched book. To play cricket one has to know the rules by heart without referring to the book every five minutes; deacons preparing for ordination to the priesthood are advised to learn the liturgy by heart, book or no book, and nowadays when all are assistant ministers that goes for everyone. Preparation for eucharistic worship becomes a quest for one's proper part: are you a batsman or a bowler or a wicket-keeper? Are you a contemplative or is your discipleship centred on discursive meditation, or have you special inter-cessory gifts? Find out first, in everyday life and prayer, and consciously bring those gifts and attitudes into the church and lay them before the altar. Are you none of those things but a practical Martha? The church accountant, or the cleaner, or the churchyard keeper? Bellringer, evangelist or pastor? Very well, bring all those things to the foot of the cross, for we are dealing with the team, including groundstaff, scorer, caterer and secretary. All the practical chores are part of the eucharistic offering.

The analogy helps again. For it will not be a successful team on Sundays unless all its members prepare for and practise their particular personal contribution throughout the previous week: eucharistic preparation is not so much a personal penitential exercise on Saturday night as a putting of the whole of life into a eucharistic context. So there has to be prayerful net-practice, accepting one's own skills, developing them and bringing it all to the match, to be placed at the disposal of the team. Preparation for public worship is private prayer.

The bikini girl brought our attention to the proper penitential element; we bring our gifts and graces but also our sins and frailties. We come to the altar naked, without pretence or apology. Everything is taken up by Christ onto the cross and into glory.

Elsewhere I have likened spiritual direction of individuals by a competent guide to coaching. Prayer is unlikely to develop satisfactorily according to *attrait* without assistance from another; not teaching, or learning, or understanding, still less commanding, but coaching – the development of personal God-given gifts and the eradication of faults and weaknesses, and sins. Seek such direction, not only, or primarily, for one's own satisfaction, for one's own spiritual progress, but for the benefit of the team. The opening batsman does not slog away at net-practice to improve his own average but to lay the foundation of a good score by the whole side.

In no other team game is individuality so conspicuous, both for good and bad, which points to some valuable teaching about aridity; the inevitable periods of spiritual dryness, dullness, boredom with prayer, general fed-upness. First and obviously, personal feelings in the daily exercise of the liturgical match are insignificant compared with the performance of the team. It is miserable to be out first ball, to have terrible bowling figures and to drop half a dozen catches. It is not much fun to feel spiritually dulled on a great festival, to let one's mind wander off at all sorts of impious tangents, to get sick and tired of this particular setting and these particular hymns. But in both cases, never mind: 'Play to win,' says St Paul in the New English Bible. So long as your team does well, why worry? It is a comforting thought for an unfortunate yet inevitable occasion.

All sportsmen come in and out of form. It is an inevitable consequence, but only in cricket are one's out-of-form periods so painfully conspicuous. After a brilliant team move the forward at football can muff a simple finishing shot, and do the same thing again and again, but it is soon forgotten with sympathetic understanding. Not quite so with a batsman whose recent scores are 0, 5, 2, 0, 1. For there it all is on paper, in the scorebook and next day in print. All Christians suffer the equivalent aridity, of being prayerfully out of form. It is a wretched state, but one which a modicum of experience and maturity learns to cope with. Perhaps we should be more open with each other, with those in the same team, on such occasions? A sympathetic team seems to work better in cricket than it does in the local church, which is a pity.

There is a subtle distinction between being out of form, playing badly, and being slothful or cheating; the latter is sinful, the former is not. Yet thousands of faithful Christians worry themselves to distraction because of aridity. They feel that their prayer is feeble, their worship lukewarm, their oblation distracted, and probably it is. It is not sinful but part of the game. For most of us seven capital sins are enough. Let us not copy Ronald Knox in his light-hearted mood by trying to invent an eighth: praying badly.

There is a moral aspect nevertheless, cheating, sharp practice, intimidation; these *are* sins, so is positive sloth, letting the side down not by being out of form but by not trying, not pulling your weight. Such sloth can be a subtle thing, for it can extend outside the actual game to lack of practice, to a slackness in trying to overcome faults. If you are a bad fielder, always missing catches to dismiss the opposing batsman, you have a duty to the team to practise, to seek spiritual direction, to seek advice, to undergo coaching. To repeat, the necessary preparation for the Sunday service is daily prayer on weekdays; the duty of all members of the team, if it is really to be a team, is to find time and energy for net-practice. It is not sufficient to turn up for the match itself and hope for the best. Daily prayer, the constant struggle against sin, is no optional extra, no private concern but a responsibility to the team: consequently, cosmic-wise, to the world. Weak worship is not sin, but sin breeds weak worship, so it needs to be eradicated – because of the team. Anglicanism is very wise about sacramental confession, but it overdoes the subjective aspect; like Guinness it is good for you. But it might become necessary to consider such glorious, joyous, lightsome discipline, for the sake of the team. Of course we are back again to athletic fasting: do not live so that you cannot chase the ball on the boundary, and it is bad for the *team* if you go in to bat half drunk.

It is so sad that modern cricket, especially the first-class variety, has succumbed to original sin according to Chesterton's definition: the devil fell through taking himself too seriously. Cricket has fallen through thinking itself too important to be enjoyed as a game. But there was a time when unfair play in any context was described as 'not cricket': those were the days. Let it be hoped that this moral element will not be entirely lost.

Cricket, like Christianity, is also of social significance, which is not quite the same as being concerned with corporate organization. Or perhaps it is the more light-hearted aspect of that corporateness. Compared with most genuine team games, a cricket match takes a long time, always several hours, sometimes several days, but it embraces meals taken together, social meetings in the evening, and tour travels. I used proudly to poke fun at the typical American church complex, with its offices, kitchens, lecture-rooms, refectory and lounge. It looked so like a plush club instead of a working church, its values and perspectives looked out of due order. But wisdom and experience have humbled me. The Episcopalians have got it right; the altar is in the middle of the church which in turn is central to the parish complex. Those churches have properly extended into the lightsome element, like a cricket team on tour.

There appears a disturbing element. A cricket team is a team because it is restricted to eleven players, no more no less, plus a few necessary helpers and administrators. St Benedict taught that the ideal liturgical congregation was about thirty; given more you go off and set up an altar elsewhere. This raises the problem of achieving true fellowship, organic *koinonia* with the sort of crowds a cathedral attracts. Should we not think again at the shallow Anglican idea that a good congregation is synonymous with the biggest possible crowd of sheep surrounded by a huge herd of goats. Parishes with a regular congregation of thirty do not know how lucky they are.

Finally, I wonder how many non-playing enthusiasts know what it feels like to go in to bat? To play for one's team but strictly as an individual with total responsibility? On the one hand here is the moment you have been waiting for, here is your chance to prove yourself, to play your innings with all the skill and enthusiasm at your disposal. On the other hand it is a terrifying experience; will you survive the first over, or the first ball? Doubtless the hardened international player of professional phlegm can carry the occasion off, but for lesser mortals it is not so comfortable. How better to describe the emotion than by the classic phrase of Dr Rudolf Otto: *Mysterium tremendum et fascinans*, the *numinous* experience which subtly combines fear with joy, comfort with terror in the presence of the Holy. Yes, you want to play your innings, you want to experience the presence of God, but it is very frightening.

Cornwall is renowned for its medieval churches, often small and remote, which nevertheless attract large numbers of tourists summer by summer. Most such churches display a visitors book, in which one is invited to sign, and these usually contain a column headed 'Remarks'. With respect, the remarks or impressions are not very original: 'Well kept', 'Beautiful', 'Quaint', or more likely 'Peaceful'. I cannot but be reminded of Jacob at Bethel: 'How fearsome is this place! This is no other than the house of God, this is the gate of heaven.' 'Truly the Lord is in this place, and I did not know it.'

So let us go into bat, let us go into the house of God to assist at the Eucharist. Let us enter with naked honesty, taking with us all that we have on behalf of the team, our gifts and skills, our sins and frailties. Let us anticipate the joys of communion with God and the team, but not, please, entirely because it is all so beautiful, peaceful and quaint. Let us also enter because it is fearful, awesome, frightening: *Mysterium tremendum et fascinans*.

Meanwhile I look forward to seeing, just once, in the remarks column of the visitors book of a remote little medieval gem, bedecked with Easter flowers: 'How dreadful is this place . . '

7
Nightmare Interlude

My recurrent nightmare grows out of a pastoral dilemma. I have hinted more than once against the prevalent habit amongst clergymen of treating their congregation, not only as an audience but as a near moronic one. In the bad old days when a congregation was regarded as a crowd of individual spectators there may have been some excuse, but with the concept of full participation within the organism of the Body of Christ such an attitude will no longer do. Traditional Anglicanism claims appeal to mature religion, to a laity who are informed and knowledgeable. Yet the idea persists: everything has to be simple, nice little moral tenets, and above all no theology.

It is a nineteenth-century trait, certainly not Carolean, and, if social circumstances partly account for it, the clergy are far from blameless. Nevertheless, the laity cannot be entirely exonerated: 'You cannot expect me to understand that, I am only a layman.' The speaker can be a high-court judge, a university professor, or chairman of a multinational company, but in church he is only a layman with a pathological terror of the word theology. And so to my nightmare, which follows on neatly from the cricket analogy. I have made apology to those readers who do not understand cricket, yet most newcomers to cricket seem to cope better than their counterparts in church. I once took two American friends to a cricket match. After just six hours, with a minimum of commentary, we had dinner where they waxed more than enthusiastic about cover point, LBW, maiden overs, off-spinners, and all the rest of the jargon. Why does it take intelligent churchfolk not six hours but six years to feel at home with redemption, grace, Pelagianism, adoration, contemplation and suchlike perfectly ordinary terms? My American friends had even picked up something about Grace, Hobbs, Woolley and Hammond: we never get around to Augustine, Anselm, Bernard and Aquinas.

So, nightmarishly, I make my way to Lords (or is it Lourdes?) and enter the Grace gates (efficacious, prevenient, sanctifying or

Dr W. G.?) I am accosted by a dapper little man wearing an I Zingari tie, presumably his badge of office for the occasion.

'Good morning, I. Z. I notice.' The official was obviously taken aback by the fact that a mere layman understood the sequence of liturgical colours.

'Yes indeed,' he replied, 'and good morning, good morning, how nice to see you, and how terribly good of you to turn up.'

I replied testily (or Testily) that I had come along at my own freewill because I wished to watch the match; I was a confirmed disciple of the game and I was doing nobody any favour.

'Of course, of course, my dear sir,' he replied, 'now you do realize, do you not – we have to assume that most of our congregation do not – that today is the third Test Match after Trinity?'

'Of course I do,' I replied, 'that is precisely what I am here for; and Australia are one up, having won the first by five wickets, the second being drawn.'

'My dear sir I do apologize,' spluttered the man in the I. Z. tie, 'I had no idea that a mere member of our congregation, a layman in fact, could be so well informed about church affairs.'

At that point he thrust into my hands a small booklet *The Rules of Cricket* together with a virgin score card.

'You will need these,' he explained, 'in order to follow the service. The Ordo, or Rule Book, has been considerably abbreviated and simplified, especially for the use of the morons . . . excuse me, the laity. I think that you might find the more definitive work (published by the Society for Promoting Cricket Knowledge) a little beyond your intellectual capacity. It contains, I regret to say, a good deal of theology, and what is worse it is apt to include slight changes from year to year. Such a pity, why cannot they leave things alone?'

'Presumably', I replied, 'because cricket is a living thing, which demands change and development according to circumstances and experience. Would you not consider the new Luther-Benedict-Wesley rule an improvement upon the old Hambledon rite?'

'I fear you have the advantage of me,' simpered my mentor.

'But surely you are *au fait* with the LBW law as recently promulgated by the Magisterium of the Cricket Council?'

'Well, perhaps you had better keep the little book by you,

despite your astounding knowledge of the service; one always needs a reminder. I strongly advise you to follow the Rule, keep your eye on the text and make sure that you *never* lose the place. Of course, you will not see much of the game, but that is a small loss compared with a thorough understanding of the theory of the thing; superstition and even emotion can so easily creep in. And dear me there goes the bell and the umpires are out: you understand about umpires? One at each end you know. Well good day, and enjoy the game, and oh your score card, you had forgotten it.'

'Thank you, but it is unnecessary . . .'

'But it has the names of the players on it . . .'

'Thank you but I know them by heart, it was all in this morning's paper.'

'My word you do take things seriously!'

In spite of this inane conversation, I managed to get a place behind the bowler's arm. Settling down happily a voice came through the amplifier; it was the Bishop of St John's Wood, cricket's chief Shepherd, and President of the MCC.

'Good morning, good morning! What a lovely day and such a large crowd. Welcome! Welcome! And how wonderful of you all to turn up. First I must announce that Australia have won the toss and elected to bat. I do not suppose that you will all understand that rather technical statement, but never mind; you are only lay spectators after all. In that case, by the way, perhaps I should offer a few words of explanation to that solid core of Cricket of England fans who do not come along very often to watch, and of course who never actually play. Quite simply the game is played between two teams of eleven players each; perhaps you might care to turn to page 6, section (b) of the rule book. The gist of the thing is that the fielding side tries to dismiss the batting side for as few runs, or points, as possible. There are various ways to dismiss a batsman: look up page 13, sections (c) to (g). But please do not feel in any way uncomfortable if you do not quite understand it all. Just follow the book and I will explain things as we go along . . .

'Now just a word to the many thousands of good churchmen who will be following the match, on and off, on the television. Now I must apologize to the majority of you but unfortunately the commentary will be given by a team of ex-professionals who will insist on talking in awful jargon: slips, cover-point, run out, leg-before-wicket, square-cut, off-drive, and a horrendous lot more. We have taken it up with the broadcasting authorities, but so far to no avail. One bumptious official had the impertinence to suggest that keen cricket-lovers ought to take the trouble to learn the meaning of all these technical terms. That is asking far too much of any enthusiast, and we will continue our crusade for simple non-theological language. In the meantime our apologies; just relax and take it easy.

'Finally, there will be two intervals during the day's play when tea and buns will be available at various centres around the ground. There was a suggestion that beer and cider might be made available but the Master of Cricket Ceremonies wisely ruled against it, not wanting to risk causing our weaker brethren to stumble. However do join in with the refreshment available, and offer friendship to your neighbour in jolly fellowship.'

Then the bell rang again, but happily it was the alarm clock. A nightmare parody, unfair, unChristian, cruel and uncharitable. But it is not so desperately far short of what happens all too often: whose fault is it?

8

The Faith in Four Days

There are many ways of observing Holy Week, ancient and
modern, traditional and experimental, all concluding with the
tremendous impact of Maundy Thursday, Good Friday, Holy
Saturday and Easter Day. An obvious and exciting thing about
these four days is their distinction in message and devotional
emphasis. What is frequently brought out less clearly is the
essential inter-relation between them; to live through these four
days is to cover the calendar, virtually to live through the creed.

Maundy Thursday is basically the day of the eucharistic
celebration, which word has its particular theological relevance.
For significantly the sacraments are administered; only the
Eucharist, in normal discourse, is celebrated. So what does the
word 'celebrate' imply?

Firstly it implies community. A desert-island castaway might
just remember his birthday – given the means to calculate it –
and drink his own health in coconut juice, but it would barely
pass as celebration. Secondly, it is based on memory of a
significant event in the past, and thirdly that event is more than
recalled, it is made present by re-enactment. The important date
as you celebrate your birthday is today, *now* you are sixty; that
you were born sixty years ago is the celebrated event, there is a
connection between the two, spanning sixty years, but it is
today, *now*, that the celebration takes place. So lastly, a celebration has to be historically based. It may be possible to conjure
up all kinds of peculiar incidents to celebrate, like falling in the
river after another celebration or being bitten by a dog, but such
events must have happened. Any excuse for a party, but you
cannot just invent a celebration. All of which, on reflection,
contains quite a bit of useful, simple, yet sound eucharistic
doctrine.

Maundy Thursday points to the family feast of the people of
God. It is more than that, much more, but the analogy of the
family meal suddenly becomes liturgically topical, offering
some illumination on current pastoral practice and experiment,

and possibly some guidance. The Eucharist is the Christian family meal; yes, but what sort of meal? Because there is more than one kind – and we could be back to sartorial conjectures about the bikini girl. Some of it is obvious enough: the heavenly banquet, high mass, with a sanctuary full of ministers dressed up with rightfully gorgeous dignity, the great family occasion, perhaps the wedding breakfast of the heir. And all properly formal, correctly ritualistic; but there are other sorts of family meals, which happen more frequently.

Good old English Sunday luncheon; roast beef and apple pie, with grandparents and a nephew or two to swell the numbers. Dom Cuthbert Butler's Benedictine ideal comes in here: love, familiarity, good manners, but no pomp or regimentation. Even the most Edwardian family does not dress for Sunday luncheon, but ties, jackets and no exposed braces gives the main thrust of the thing. This is the Sung Eucharist on a normal Sunday, bikini girl notwithstanding.

Then there is what Mrs Beeton calls that comfortable meal called breakfast; the quiet little celebration early in the morning. And supper which is nearly but not quite the same, only in the evening. What of the house-mass? Assuredly the shirtsleeves and carpet slippers affair round the family hearth, with little pomp and a minimum of ceremony.

The point of the analogy is that the riches of the eucharist are too much to absorb at one go, and we may be missing out by a bigoted insistence on a single type. The numinous wonder of the old high mass, eastward position and eastern altar, pointing to the majesty of the Holy Trinity; the domesticity of the ferial central altar; the so-special occasion demanding serious preparation, and the straight low-key celebration which is the Christian's normal daily food, the simple family meal. Perhaps parishes and people might benefit by switching the devotional emphases around?

Maundy Thursday remains the day of eucharistic celebration, the re-enactment or making present of the passion, which points to the incarnation. So to the cross.

You cannot be light-hearted before the cross. But you can be, and ultimately must be, unsentimental and theologically aware, and the secret of Good Friday devotion is an attempt at a synthesis between what tradition knows as the objective and subjective theories of the atonement. To sum up, we seek a subjective approach to an objective fact: 'When I survey the wondrous Cross'.

The initial approach on Good Friday has to be unashamed nakedness, prostration; the woodlouse has to roll itself up into a ball of surrender. The crucified, atoning woodlouse incarnate. The physical sufferings of Jesus are treated in hundreds of devotional classics, not least in that sublime devotional–theological synthesis in the ninth *Revelation* of Julian of Norwich: 'Then said Jesus our kind Lord: If thou art pleased, I am pleased: it is a joy, a bliss, an endless satisfying to me that ever suffered I passion for thee; and if I might suffer more, I would suffer more.'

It would be foolish to try to improve on this meditation, except possibly to show the inadequacy of the woodlouse analogy at this point. It can be assumed that physical suffering increases with human sensitivity, our own sufferings are more acute than those of a woodlouse in the fire, and the sacred humanity of Jesus implies a greater sensitivity than we can imagine. Yet this means little compared with the spiritual agony of the sinless suffering which is the price of sin: 'My God, My God, why hast thou forsaken me.'

Yet the cross is a wondrous one; it is the supreme victory, and on the grounds that nobody will achieve the ultimate synthesis – with the possible exception of Julian and St Anselm – it comes down to the question of *attrait*. So we should not be ashamed if our meditation on the passion fails to stir our affections as truly as we should wish. It is more important to cling fast to the objective fact of atonement once for all achieved. 'O sacred head sore wounded' has to be balanced by 'Sing my tongue the glorious battle'.

I do not think that I am alone in being a little disturbed by military parade services, because the only posture suitable before the cross is naked prostration, not standing proudly to attention with personal decorations flapping. Yet if we are at the cross with St Anselm, or with Julian, perhaps a modicum of flag-waving might be permissible: 'It is finished,' the victory is complete. Christ ascended the cross naked and yet 'the royal banners forward go'. An ancient liturgical tradition sees Good Friday as a non-liturgical day, with no music, hymns, congregational meditations or whatever. Just prostration plus naked joy at the foot of the cross. It is a pity that this tradition has been overruled, and it could hint at a return of the cricketing nightmare: have the laity got to be stimulated and talked at all the time? Are the faithful incapable of one day's holy silence?

Or rather two days. Because if there is a day of contemplative silence within the Christian year it must be Holy Saturday, or Easter Eve, or the Greater Sabbath. The original sabbath indicates God's outpouring of contemplative love sustaining the completed creation. The second, or Greater Sabbath, is characterized by Christ's contemplative love consummating creation's redemption; the whole creation, all four divisions of the Thomist league.

On Easter Day all but the grizzliest puritan want our churches and cathedrals to be bedecked with colour and flowers and music, indicating the victory of Christ for creation. But must we all start bustling about at nine o'clock on the Greater Sabbath morning? Having made the penitential gesture of austerity for the forty days of Lent, what a pity to spoil it all right at the end. And it is playing into Screwtape's hand, for there are three things that the devil can neither achieve nor tolerate: prayer, silence, and sitting still.

There are many classic analogies for the resurrection: the grain of corn that has to die and be buried in order to rise and bear fruit through transformation. The Easter egg which, being broken, brings embryonic life out into a wider, more expansive environment.

Christianity teaches the doctrine of the resurrection of the body, which is so distinct from the philosophical notion of the immortality of the soul. That is why I have aways been suspicious of the word 'soul', either in theology or more especially in devotion: it tends to become either ambiguous or sentimental. Neither do I feel at home with the Quaker's divine spark, or the life-principle, or similar phrases. Yet what does one make of Christ's resurrection as of cosmic significance, as affecting all four divisions of the Thomist football league, in this context? And how is this squared with God's personal love for the woodlouse and for Sister Milly the millipede?

It is a hoary old idea that, explain it how you like, by physics or chemistry or physiology, there remains some indefinable and wondrous thing called *life*, which must be indestructible because if the resurrection is of cosmic significance, then everything is indestructible. It was brought home to me a couple of years ago when I nearly died, and watched a woodlouse wandering round the bean plants exuding nitrogen, volatile plant nutrient: *life*.

In spite of the great Albert Schweitzer, neither have I been entirely happy with the morality centred on the sanctity of life, especially as it pertains to emotive subjects like euthanasia, capital punishment and pacifism. Let me hasten to add that I have no intention to cut my throat, that I have no desire to hang anyone, and I do not want to start a war: I simply do not find the sanctity of life arguments very convincing. It is simply that, if we take the doctrine of the resurrection of Jesus seriously, human life here in the third division is less, not more, important. After all St Paul was bewildered: 'to be with Christ which is much better.' He was willing to stay in the third division if he could be useful, but he was more anxious to get into the second with all the other saints. It is a peculiar embryo duck that does not want to be hatched.

It is central to the gospel that Jesus did not have to die; he chose to. And what happens to the Christian tradition of the glorious company of martyrs?

But back to Milly and the woodlouse: no immortality of the soul, no divine spark, above all no death, because the last enemy is overcome. 'Sing my soul the glorious battle.' That is the Easter mystery: let us rejoice.

I have hinted that these four days summarize the whole of Christian living based on the whole creed: Maundy Thursday has the Eucharist based on the incarnation; Good Friday is atonement–redemption day; Holy Saturday is the contemplative consummation of the redeemed creation; the whole cosmic universe is resurrected on Easter Day.

These four days depict the fundamental progression of the Christian life of prayer, a progression of three stages, or aspects of prayer, which nevertheless continue to interplay throughout the whole of life, however advanced that life may become. The three stages start with the covenant relation between God and humankind which means obedience to the divine command. Maundy Thursday is all about simple obedience: 'Do this in remembrance of me'; never mind the theory, stop fussing about worthiness of reception; *do it*.

Good Friday is also about obedience, that of Christ on the cross, the final consummation of the covenant with the Father. The next stage is our *encounter* with the resurrected Lord, our relation with God transformed from simple obedience to his commands to a living personal relationship. That is one reason why, whatever our *attrait*, however lacking in affective devotion, meditation on the cross and passion, centred on the Sacred Humanity, cannot be left out. Without the resurrection, the Easter message, there can be no meeting with Jesus.

Finally there is *incorporation* into that Sacred Humanity; the grafting of human buds into the divine parent-stock: the stupendous hope of our deification, or as Teilhard would have it, christification. This is what St Paul means by being 'in Christ', and it is the contemplative stage; back to Maundy Thursday and on again to Easter Day.

If that is the fundamental schema of Christian life – covenant, encounter, incorporation – it is to be noted that it forms both progression and pattern. In other words we move from obedience to awareness of Christ's presence to contemplation of and in his resurrected life. It is trinitarian and eucharistic. But in another sense all the stages overlap and interact throughout life; we never grow out of the need for simple obedience to divine commandment.

For the sake of completeness, and at some risk of repetition, I shall now add three post-Easter summaries, spelling out the process and pattern in a little more detail, and forming some sort of précis to the rest of the book.

9

Eastertide Wedding

There is a sense in which Lent books, courses and rules have an autonomous value; Holy Week may be seen as ten rounds of the boxing match, the final fight perhaps on our devotional Good Friday. The Greater Sabbath is the contemplative consummation of the victory, with Easter Day as its great celebration. Then in a sense it is all over, but in another sense it is just beginning. It is to be hoped that our ascetical preparation for the fight, the total fasting programme, will result in an increased and deepened faith for the rest of our lives, if after a proper and well earned post-Easter rest.

There are many traditional analogies for living this total and continuous Christian life, while central to them all is the classic nuptial-domestic one, centred on the notion of the Church as the Bride of Christ, and as the Family of God. The analogical implications of this are inexhaustible, moving between the subtlest theology of deification, christification and the mystical marriage, to the simplest pastoral custom like referring to the priest as Father and seeing the Eucharist under the metaphor of the family meal.

The nuptial analogy is practically indispensable in pastoral teaching on prayer, and there is hardly a major saint who has not employed it in some form or another. In spite of all this it might be worth looking at it again, lightsomely, by way of general summary, as an attempt to bring together some of the ideas and little bits of counsel this book has tried to deal with; to extend it all beyond Lent and Easter and look at Christian life as a whole continuum. It is admittedly repetitive and yet the very elements of creative prayer cannot be repeated too often, and even among the advanced it is the elements that tend to be overlooked, swallowed up in a tangled mass of spiritual–theological sophistication.

Discounting all the ramifications of conversion, Christian life and prayer begins with baptism, and it can start nowhere else; this in itself is a common example of overlooking the obvious.

For baptism is analogous to our marriage to Christ, both personally and corporately. The Church is the Bride of Christ; so is the sister in the professed religious life, so is the brother, and so are you and me. By baptism we are married to Christ, incorporated, taken up into the Sacred Humanity, engrafted into the parent vine, to live upon its life-blood. There can be no other starting point, and constant consideration of this fact, this freely given status, is fundamental to a healthy spirituality. Aspire to the higher contemplative states, achieve the ultimate union of the mystical marriage, but it is all founded on baptism.

Let us spell out the analogy in some detail, but only as a beginning of a continuous spelling it out for ourselves. Marriage is permanent, unbreakable, and it forms a continuous relationship. It is given not earned and, to return to the fundamental pattern looked at in the last chapter, it embraces covenant, encounter, and incorporation. It is a covenant because on its lowest level it is a contract demanding loyalty and obedience, it has a strong moral element but this is far from the heart of the matter. It is encounter because it implies a living relationship between two people, one of great complexity with all kinds of expression and degrees of intimacy. But mystically the two people are not two but one, the twain shall be one. Life and prayer in its sublime Christian simplicity is to obey Christ, to meet Christ, and to be in Christ – and he in us.

So the first point about Christian prayer is that it is a given status in which we are, and the first practical exercise in it is to develop a recollective awareness, even a subconscious awareness, that this is so. Two partners in marriage can be a thousand miles apart and wholly wrapped up in different absorbing activities, but it does not make any difference to the underlying relationship: they are still married. We can be as devotionally arid as the desert, wholly engaged in some vital enterprise of a practical kind, stretching all our faculties to the limit, but we are still at, or in, prayer even if we are not consciously praying: we cannot be unbaptized. But this is no comfortable theory, no sentimental *laborare est orare* nonsense, for to pray, as against being in a state of prayer, means positive response to the eternal status, and this by numerous means.

Colloquy is a composite word for informal – hence colloquial – spiritual dialogue, generally sub-divided into adoration, confession, intercession and supplication. The day-to-day conversation between man and wife, me and God. Again the involved relation is more important than its content; dialogue forges a relation and expresses a union, never mind what it is about. In more gracious days social intercourse centred around the 'art of conversation'. The subject did not matter much so long as the dialogue was stimulating and interesting. That is what our prayerful conversation with Jesus ought to be, stimulating and interesting. Two people can converse lovingly, adoringly, or practically, about the bills and blocked-up drains, or as intercession, concerning the needs of others – 'and especially those that are of the household of faith'. The nuptial analogy puts a fresh and exciting complexion on saying your prayers.

In marriage, confession and absolution follows upon in-evitable quarrels, and it is the keynote of domestic harmony; but good as it may be for two people to confess or admit their failings one to another, and offer mutual forgiveness, it is even more effective when it is arranged that both are forgiven by God.

Such simple colloquy, never to be despised, and much enlightened by the nuptial–domestic analogy, will be looked at again in the following chapter.

There is a marital meditation, the quiet, discursive, thinking things out together, with or without a lot of words. It is the daily solving of mutual problems, the daily means of enlightening and deepening the underlying relationship. May it continue to be remembered that this prayer, like all prayer, remains primarily about the relationship, not about solving problems. Christ enters the marital relation as he entered the world; not so much to alleviate suffering as to share it. The analogy immedi-ately eliminates a great deal of prevalent naivety: does God answer prayer? why does this happen to me? surely God . . ., etc. Consider the analogy, and a great many so-called 'difficulties in prayer' vanish into thin air.

There is marital contemplation, a simple speechless being together, and how subtle it can be. Here is the normal ultimate of spiritual experience; simply to be in the presence of God – and we are warned against the liturgical idolatry of the book: you neither read nor think in the presence of God. The husband–

wife team need not think or speak either, they need simply to be; the prayer of loving regard as it is sometimes called. Or they can hold hands, or embrace, which points to the contemplative outlook of such as St Mary Magdalene, who never said much but neither was she entirely satisfied with the simple loving glance. She needed bodily contact, the wider sacramentalism, the caressing of the sacred feet with tears and her hair down.

'I love you' could be a non-intellectual contemplative *mantra*, after the pattern of the Jesus Prayer; while any symbol could provide a mutual *mandala*, a picture or crucifix, clover leaf or triangle, or for that matter a woodlouse or a lobster. If two in love sit before their fireside in contemplative awareness, then the fire itself may be a very important accessory to the exercise.

Laborare est orare – to work is to pray – is conducive to sentimentality, even worse to spiritual sloth, because the fundamental baptismal relation, the marriage to Christ, is no easy option: like all deep relationships of love it has to be worked at. There has to be positive and disciplined response. Yet there is a sense in which it is true. Practical mutual service, complementary work, shared interests, can all be part of the relationship, therefore of prayer, when, and only when, the baptismal marriage with Christ is accepted, absorbed, and continuously worked out.

'. . . for better for worse, for richer for poorer, in sickness and in health . . .' It all has its analogical interpretation to the life of prayer. Sometimes our meditation is better, sometimes worse, but it should not interfere with the basic relationship. By grace our devotion can be rich, often it is poor, and it does not really matter. We have overcome the stupidity of trying to invent the eighth capital sin; it is unfortunate, even painful, when our prayer is poorer and worse, but barring positive sloth, it cannot be sinful.

We can be spiritually sick, and morally sick, and yet neither of these states need be sinful. What is certain is that any such sickness can never separate us from the love of God in Christ Jesus because nothing can break the baptismal marriage bond.

Many of the lustier saints of the Middle Ages had no hesitation or embarrassment in likening the sexual-sacramental aspect of marriage – significantly referred to as its consummation – with the act of Holy Communion. And the analogous implications are obvious enough. Here the twain are one flesh, in a mutual self-giving which is a mutual and creative life-giving. In New Testament times blood is assumed to be, or to contain, the life-force: 'This is my blood' means this is my life. The divine life of the crucified actually, literally, flowing into our own bloodstreams: deification, christification. As our English fourteenth-century asceticists so succinctly put it, we are *oned* with God.

The nuptial analogy is inexhaustible, and the foregoing is only a start. Readers are invited to carry on for themselves, for apart from the central theme of prayer as continuous, living relationship with God in Christ and Christ in us, it exposes and eliminates a good deal of theological difficulty. Twenty years ago or thereabouts Bishop John Robinson caused something of a stir with *Honest to God*, exploding the myth of God seen crudely as object, 'out there'. It was a valuable contribution in the translation of doctrine from the old substantive categories – what is God made of? what are his attributes? – to an existential standpoint, how is God experienced as Being? 'I am that I am . . . before Abraham was, I am.'

But many sensed a snag, a vague feeling of dissatisfaction in this sort of thinking. Without great theological expertise a weakness was intuited by many of the faithful. The snag and weakness is that, while discounting the crudity of a divine object in the form of an old gentleman sitting on a cloud, the existential concept must be brought into a trinitarian context; in other words we cannot eliminate the transcendental element. In a sense God the Father is 'out there', wholly other, utterly independent of this world and its affairs. He is beyond the first division, let alone the third. And it is better to see this transcendent element in a crude spatial imagery than not at all.

All this is explained and put to rights by the nuptial analogy enframed within the basic three-fold pattern of spiritual progress. In practice there has always to be a covenant relation as well as one of encounter and incorporation. The almighty Father, incomprehensible and majestic, gives commands which have to be obeyed, and no amount of mystical expertise will eliminate the need for such obedience. To be married to Christ by baptism assumes the good-will of the Father almighty.

So we have an overall pattern for Christian life and spiritual advancement: covenant–obedience, encounter, and incorporation–marriage. All of which, inevitably, is both trinitarian and eucharistic. The family, behind the nuptial analogy, is itself a trinitarian symbol: mother, father, child. And the basic three-fold pattern is summed up in eucharistic worship. The ministry of the word, lections and their exposition, points to obedience to the covenant; consecration induces encounter with the resurrected Christ sacramentally present; and Holy Communion is the ultimate consummation of the baptismal wedding: incorporation, or Christ in us and we in him.

10

Biblical Encounters

The events of Jesus' public ministry can be, and have been, interpreted in many ways; as theology, as pastoral guidance, as of moral implication, as introduction to the mind of Christ. It has not been so readily seen that any account of his meeting with others, especially in an individual situation, comprises teaching about prayer – what we have called the stage of encounter. Such prayer follows naturally upon the primary stage of a covenant relation with God by obedience.

In the Old Testament, characterized throughout by some facet of this covenant relation, it is generally expressed in a social or communal context. Through the prophets God gives universal laws applicable to the overall vocation of the chosen people. Yet such laws go deeper than social or personal morality. When we speak somewhat glibly about divine law or commandment, we are apt to get bogged down in a superficial ethic, forgetting that God's covenant embraces very much more: natural truth, even metaphysical truth, ritual practice, social justice, and above all liturgical regulation. Although ultimately indissociable, God's covenant with the human race is more about right worship than right conduct or right belief. In other words it is about religion, our overall relation with God himself.

In the New Testament, the sphere of the prayer of encounter, obedience becomes more personal, the universal covenant is elaborated into personal commands issuing out of a meeting, a dialogue, with Christ himself. The obvious example is the dominical command, 'Follow me', accepted by St Matthew but tragically rejected by the rich young ruler. So the first principle of this prayer of encounter, ordinary simple vocal conversation with the Lord, is to listen rather than talk, and his encounters with the various New Testament characters give us the clue as to the sort of answers he is likely to give, to the type of personal command we might expect. The encounter and dialogue between Christ and others, of all sorts and in every kind of situation, covers pretty well every possible circumstance in our spiritual pilgrimage.

The purpose of this chapter is to examine some of these stories just to give a taste, a few examples, as to how we might learn to improve our daily vocal prayer by meditating on Christ's dealings with others. First, as a general background principle, let us look at the story of Zacchaeus, who played hide-and-seek with the Lord (Luke 19. 1–10).

Prayer has been defined as our response to our baptismal status, as recognition of our incorporation into, or marriage with Jesus. It is a status we are given, not one that we acquire, so response to encounter with Christ implies that he always holds the initiative. We do not seek God, but recognize and respond to the fact that he has found us. It is Christ who does the searching. How well little Zacchaeus saw the point! He was rich and influential, but that gave him no privileged right to barge in on the Lord of all: pray excuse my canonical dignity. But he was also small of stature, no doubt literally, but perhaps in spirit as well? He may have been one of those thousands of layfolk who honestly claim no great gifts of the spirit, who found prayer and devotion difficult. That is true humility, but he did not turn it into sloth by making an excuse not to try: I cannot cope with the liturgy too often so I go for something simpler. Little, rich, short-of-stature Zacchaeus sought to see Jesus.

He did not thrust forward himself or his position, he did not seek a confrontation with Jesus, he did not get in his way: he got out of it. He went on ahead and got himself in the best possible position for the Lord to find him; he climbed a tree, setting his sights high despite disability, and waited. We are back with fasting, lenten or otherwise. For we have defined fasting as that total ascetical discipline, mental, physical, emotional, which supports our actual prayer, which puts us in God's way, initiates our response to his invitation.

Jesus passed by that way, looked up at the tree and found him. Zacchaeus did not find Jesus, Jesus found him, and yet Zacchaeus had played his necessary part. He did not grandly invite the Lord into his house, he waited for the Lord to invite himself, and received him joyfully, sinner that he was. Then he explained himself in humble simplicity; I give lots of alms to the poor, and I deal with scrupulous honesty: boasting? self-justification? Certainly not for this is the obverse side of true humility, of being honest about one's gifts as well as one's failings, of thanking God for making Zacchaeus Zacchaeus and not someone else: no angelism here, no mealy-mouthed mock modesty. Honest humility.

On the whole, however, it looks as if Zacchaeus was at heart a good honest practical man, a conscientious tax man, with no great pretensions to the mystical heights. He did not justify himself by his moral works; he just explained the facts, while admitting to a smallness of stature in all ways. Yet today salvation came to his house, he attained redemption, not as a contemplative but as a tax-collector, like the honest church-treasurer who does his vocational job without pretence. But the secret is the same for both; they are justified not as honest artisans with no great spiritual gifts, but as members of the team. It was not as a loyal disciple or a giver of alms, or as a decent fellow at heart that Zacchaeus found salvation, but as a son of Abraham, one within the corporate whole.

It has been noted that the prayer of encounter, or colloquy, is often divided into adoration, supplication, confession and thanksgiving. It is a handy framework, yet the emphasis of personal prayer is frequently placed on supplication, itself sub-divided into petition and intercession; the one seeking divine favour for oneself and one's own, the other seeking favour on behalf of others. It has been maintained by some eminent writers, notably Friedrich Heiler and H. H. Farmer, that supplication is the very core of personal devotion. It is certainly true today that, on a conversational plane, most Christians of all types and abilities, immediately think of vocal prayer as intercession. There is certainly plenty of petition and inter-cession in the New Testament by those in encounter with Jesus, but if we look back to the nuptial analogy in the last chapter, this assessment needs revision.

The prayer of encounter, colloquy, is essentially an ex-pression of a marital relationship with Jesus, it is exciting conversation, creative dialogue, and such relational qualities are scarcely applicable to petition or the straightforward asking for favours. Please dear, will you give me a new frock; please dear, do you mind if I pop off to the pub for a drink with the boys, is barely the basis for interesting conversation. How can we help old Harry? may be a loving intercessory question, but again it is barely conversation. We are back to the naivety of a relationship with God in Christ consisting entirely of our request and his answer. Let us look at the glorious dialogue between Jesus and the woman of Samaria (John 4. 7–30).

The meeting between Christ and the woman was fortuitous; unlike Zacchaeus she neither expected nor planned this encounter, in fact it took her by surprise. Then, rather than receiving her petition Jesus makes his own to her: give me a drink. St John's irony has its humorous side, it is lightsome, yet deeply christological, for the divine giver of the water of life is humanly thirsty. We are rid of two heretical birds with one stone. Now the encounter turns out to be not only unsought but socially unacceptable; Jews, expecially rabbis, have no dealings with Samaritans – you can hardly expect dignified canons and well-dressed churchwardens to have anything to do with girls in bikinis.

Then comes a very funny muddled-up conversation about water and its theological symbolism. How muddled the poor lady is! Jesus explains the facts without delivering a theological lecture, or even preaching a sermon. The woman does not ask for the living water of life until she is prodded into it by Jesus; he offers it, it is his initiative because it always is. This prayer, dialogue, encounter is *not* petition. It is conversation, a gradual deepening of a relationship.

Then comes the woman's marital tangle, which is subject to subtle social-theological interpretation, but in our meditative context let us settle for the fun of the thing; lightsome banter, and what a meal of it Jesus made! Ah, but it all inevitably leads to some deep theological teaching about worship; personal prayer always returns to the liturgy, there can be no other outcome.

Unlike Zacchaeus the woman asked for nothing, either for herself or for others, this is not petition or intercession, but what marvellous *prayer*. In common with Zacchaeus the Samaritan woman accepted the initiative of Jesus all the time; both were willing to await the outcome and act upon it. Zacchaeus accepted salvation for himself and his household. The woman was called to proclaim the gospel to her friends and neighbours: 'Come, see a man who told me all that I ever did. Can this be the Christ?'

The glory of the story is that, putting aside for the moment its topical ecclesiastic and doctrinal implications, it is not really a story *about* anything: simply a nineteenth-century *conversazione*, a means for people to get to know one another better. It is so much more exciting than 'Please God solve my problem', or even 'Please solve someone else's'.

This does not mean that simple petition or intercession is to be discounted, for it can still forge relationship and enlighten that relationship. Look, for example, at the Canaanite woman (Matthew 15. 21–8).

Here is direct emotional intercession, to which Jesus refused to listen. True prayer goes ill with panic, and the woman, naturally distressed as she was, got equally short shrift from the disciples; Jesus did not answer her a word, and the disciples begged him to send her away; what an intolerable nuisance she was! But they were not all that hard-hearted. Christ had theological reasons, reasons of principle, for not having his true mission interrupted by Canaanites. The message went home, and the first panicky outburst gave way to more reasonable prayer: softly 'Lord help me', no emotional gesticulation, for that is what one imagines, but humble supplication on her knees. Then the delightful argument, where it looks as if the Son of God gets the worst of it and gives in. No doubt he held the initiative all the time, and knew perfectly well what the outcome would be. But Jesus was never content to be a universal provider, uncle God of the agony column, he wanted relationship nurtured by faith and love, which was his achievement not that of the Canaanite lady. What wonderful pastoral technique! And what instruction for us: intercession for others, petition for oneself, but no panic and do not be frightened to argue with the Lord. He would appear to prefer argument to servility, and dialogue to results. Had the girl died all would not have been lost, in fact nothing would have been lost: how immeasurably valuable is unanswered prayer. (Has this an ecumenical message? Can the cause of unity be hastened by Anglicans being lax and disloyal Anglicans, or by Methodists giving up their distinctive tradition? United services cannot displace either the Eucharist or pure Wesleyan worship. Let us be friendly with the Canaanites but not at the expense of mutual integrity.)

All the petitionary stories have their special message, their particular nuance. Look at Nicodemus (John 3.1–21). Here is straight theological teaching, but offered in the most intimate secret dialogue; how often must students – of all sorts and conditions – be reminded that prayer is the only consummation of doctrinal studies, for prayer and doctrine are but two sides of the same coin. The end of a careful meditation on the first portion of the Athanasian Creed has to be the contemplation of a trinitarian *mandala*.

Or look at the marriage at Cana, with its comic, and cosmic, hint at the divinity of Jesus, and an even subtler hint at the humorous humanity breaking through his relation with his mother. How utterly trite for the commentators to explain that Jesus is not really being rude to the Blessed Virgin! Why do we all so easily forget that she, too, is human, and that she too enjoys a bit of fun.

The story of the unjust judge (Luke 18.1–8) reminds us again of the Canaanite woman, for both centre around the sort of petition that involves argument with the Lord, even pestering him; it all comes back to relationship rather than results.

In Mark 10.35–45, James and John come surreptitiously along to Jesus seeking favoured positions in the coming kingdom, and this follows on Christ's direct confrontation with the blushing twelve, well caught out in discussing which of them was to be the greatest (Mark 9.33–7). Jesus offers teaching about real not superficial greatness, about the greatness of humility, but the dialogue carries wider, more general teaching about the prayer of supplication itself. Not only may our relation with the Lord be strengthened by argument, but there can be no restriction on its subject matter. In the rather tight and tense approach of some of our seventeenth-century Anglican forebears, there was argument about the 'proper' subjects of prayer; what could one pray for and what ought to be avoided? And it got a little casuistical in the popular but wrong sense of that misused word; you could ask God for good health but not for social distinction, you could petition for blessings on crops and herds but not directly for financial profit.

The point about these Markan passages is that, not only can you talk to Jesus about privileged places in the coming kingdom, but if you did not he would force you to: 'What were you discussing on the way?' The results of such petitions might be anything, but very likely negative, as in these cases, but again it does not matter. It is the forging, the consolidating, of the total relationship with the Lord that really counts. In spite of constant repetition we still forget that prayer is directed to '. . . God, unto whom all hearts be open, all desires known, and from whom no secrets are hid . . .' So what is the point of trying to cover up the grizzly truth? Go to God in Christ and have it out.

If all these confrontations between Jesus and others point to a glorious diversity of petitionary relationship, the same goes for the confession–forgiveness encounter. St Mary Magdalene is the penitent *par excellence*, the classic example of utter love with few words, contemplative worship with no holds barred; self-surrender and absolute honesty. If there are two extra special characteristics about Mary's penitence it is her utter self-giving and complete generosity, illustrated, or symbolized by her tears and by the affair of the precious ointment. She let her hair down, and held nothing back. She was also the classic example of that particular contemplative whose prayer is tied to creation, to sign and symbol. She will have nothing to do with the quest for pure spirit, for angelism, because her body, her senses, her physical passion were all part of her prayer, and all part of her penitential oblation. The commentators explain how the ointment episode has prophetic links with the Lord's death, as indeed our Lord himself interprets it. But there is a minor symbol in the lavishness of the gesture. This was precious stuff, and Mary made no polite liturgical gesture; she flung it around, she threw it away.

Compare this with the story of the man born blind, in John 9.1–12, with its elaborate sacramental ritual, bodily healing being linked with forgiveness of sin. Here more significance is given to the spiritual value of material things, clay and dust and spittle, and then the Pool of Siloam. The woman with the haemorrhage was cured, and forgiven – loosed from the clutches of Satan – by touching the hem of Christ's garment. The centurion's servant was cured, forgiven, from afar. All the stories have their own special emphasis; penitence and forgiveness flow from encounter and the experience is so rich.

Lastly there is the woman caught in the act of adultery (John

7.53–8.11). You cannot be light-hearted about the cross, neither can you be easy-going about the sin that led to it, and yet here even the Son of God appears to be subjecting the pharisaic accusers to a dose of the divine humour!

In this context there are many other stories, all bringing out the riches of encounter with the living Lord, all deal with relationship, but we can hardly omit the Pharisee and the Publican in (Luke 18.9–14). It sums it all up.

Here is some attempt to bring out some of the particular elements in the prayer of personal encounter, in ordinary vocal prayer – petition, intercession, confession. Thanksgiving also has its personal side, linked as it must be with the adoration of the blessed Trinity, always the peak of Christian living, always the ultimate in human achievement.

But here the personal and the corporate come together, flowing into one another, and while granting its personal impact it is in the liturgy that adoration is ultimately expressed. Let us now summarize the odd little hints and suggestions on liturgical devotion that have cropped up throughout the book.

11
Liturgical Summary

Thanksgiving is an essential element in personal prayer which should eventually flow into adoration, the ultimate peak. But it is not surprising that the ultimate peak of perfection in anything is never easy to achieve. However we are considerably helped by the fact that, as the personal and corporate here flow into one another, the discipline of the divine office comes to our assistance. The office is essentially corporate, it is the prayer of the Church offered to the Father, through the Son and in the Holy Spirit, and even when recited in solitude it is still the Church's trinitarian offering and never a private devotion. However dull and inadequate our offering may appear, our deficiency is made up by our baptismal incorporation into Christ, by our joining in with the perpetual offering of the whole Church, saints and the hierarchy of heaven as well. In other words the divine office, properly understood and objectively given, is an ideal preparation for eucharistic worship. It is Christ-charged adoration that we are unable to achieve by ourselves.

Here we are concerned, not so much with liturgical theology but with practical attitudes, with a psychological approach and volition, in preparation for and then participation in, the Eucharist itself. Let us first look at four basic principles which underlie eucharistic worship, and which in conventional language might be called remote preparation.

First, although we are concerned here with practical techniques rather than liturgical doctrine, the more background understanding of eucharistic theology the better. And, for goodness sake, let us be neither disturbed nor frightened of it! Let us once and for all throw off the nightmare detailed in chapter 7. Let us lightsomely recognize that theology is fun. Contemporary liturgical studies have created a veritable revolution in understanding and practice, so let us throw over for ever the lay inferiority-complex with which we have been bogged down for far too long and struggle a little with the background knowledge as to what the Eucharist is. Whatever it is its ultimate meaning transcends the intellectual, and there always have been gifted Christians who intuit the truth without being capable of articulating it. I believe that this is, in fact, the state we find in many a devout communicant today; those who would be hard-pressed to give any rational explanation of eucharistic doctrine but who, deep down, know perfectly well what is going on. Nevertheless some minimum intellectual foundation is necessary, or at least useful.

Secondly, let us give proper emphasis to the corporate aspect, indicated by our various references to the team-game analogy, especially in chapters 3 and 6. Yes, there is also an intensely individualistic aspect as well – to be considered shortly – and it is always difficult to get the balance just right, but in modern circumstances this is exaggerated at the expense of the communal. We *assist* at the Eucharist, we participate in it; we are never spectators.

Thirdly, there is another difficult balance to achieve, that between the immanent and transcendent, or the subjective and objective. The Eucharist is very much a matter of God entering our world, of Christ 'coming down' to redeem and feed us, but it is also a question of our world being 'taken up' into the heavenly realm. As the Athanasian Creed puts it, 'One, not by conversion of the Godhead into flesh: but by taking of the Manhood into God.' Eucharistically 'One, not by conversion of the Godhead into bread: but by taking of the Breadhood into God.' That neither denies the humanity of Jesus nor the objective presence of Christ in the sacred elements, but it stresses the transcendent aspect; the lifting up as well as the coming down. I have attempted to bring out the point in chapters 3 and 4.

Fourthly, it follows that, having established the transcendent element, this must issue further into the cosmic element, as treated in chapter 3, and which forms the main burden of the epistle to the Colossians. Inevitably there is another paradox to resolve; the church local *is* local, concerned with the minutiae of everyday things in very ordinary places, with the day-to-day ups and downs of each member of a little society. Yet our worship is tragically impoverished if we neglect its cosmic significance, which is far more than intercessory concern for far-flung places in our little planet, important as that may be in its place. Chapter 3 attempted to explain.

I do not for a moment claim that these four points or principles offer a comprehensive account of eucharistic doctrine, but they seem especially important in the present pastoral climate, and lead into some very practical aspects of preparation. Meanwhile the more that orthodox doctrine can be studied and absorbed the clearer things will be. In order to achieve down-to-earth brevity, and I hope simplicity, I have summarized the foregoing teaching in bluntly pedagogic vein, as simple and direct instruction. If this appears to be unfashion- ably paternalistic I apologize, and yet what is the point of being called Father if one is not permitted a little gentle paternalism? So, to improve on our eucharistic performance, to deepen and enrich our worship, what do we do? How do we prepare?

First, as ministers of the sacrament, not spectators or audience, it is necessary to *learn the framework and structure of the rite by heart*. For a large majority of communicants this is superfluous advice, for even a new rite becomes committed to memory very soon; a dozen celebrations will usually do the trick. But supplement this by praying the invariable prayers in private, or even learning them by rote.

Secondly, then *throw away the book*. We are there to worship God and perform our cosmic duty, not to get buried in printed words. We saw in chapter 6 that you do not go in to bat with the rules of cricket in your pocket, to be consulted at the end of each over to make sure that you know what is going on.

Thirdly, self-examination in preparation for Holy Com- munion ought to be what it says it is – self-examination – and not only the unearthing and confession of sin. It should be, as the *Imitation of Christ* has it: 'a humble knowledge of thyself as a surer way to God than a deep search after learning'. Humility we have seen is a complete and honest acceptance of the gifts and graces that God has bestowed as well as their spoliation by our sin. This is necessary because nothing less than our honest self in total is to be brought into the church and laid at the foot of the cross. Looking back at the past week, for the Eucharist is retrospective as well as anticipatory, we attempt to uncover our sins but also to rejoice in our successes, in our merits and accomplishments, with thanksgiving for grace bestowed. It has to be a total oblation for the whole of life, which once offered leaves us prostrate and naked before the Lord. That was the burden of the open and honest bikini girl in chapter 5, and a final condemnation of our vain attempt to appear before Christ clothed with pseudo-respectability.

The analogy in chapter 6 asks us to try to discover exactly what our fundamental gifts are, or what it is that makes up our vocation. Have we contemplative gifts? or *attrait* for intercession? Have we a clear thirst for meditation on the divine wisdom, or an affective and properly emotional devotion towards the sacred and suffering humanity? Or have we none of these things? Just a gift for figures that makes us into a good church treasurer, or a flair for flower arranging, or the laundering of linen, or for singing in the choir? It matters not what it is but all, everything, has to be accepted and brought and offered, never forgetting our sins. Then we are naked, then we may give up and give in. Only now do we communicate worthily, because there is no pretence, no artificial tension, nothing to get in the way of our nakedness, not even sartorial convention.

Fourthly, I have suggested, in chapter 8, that our worship might be enriched by making preparation according to the type of celebration we are to be involved in. The emphases are different as between the Sunday parochial service, with its ceremonial and music, and the simple said celebration on ferial mornings. There are both similarities and differences between a test match and cricket on the village green. Perhaps the former is rather more of the team game, more obviously the offering of the corporate whole; the latter less formal and more personal. The first is the family meal, the social occasion marking a significant aspect of family life; the second is the health-giving snack, the ordinary daily sustenance. Let it be insisted again, with Dom Cuthbert Butler, that neither is a military parade; just sufficient formality is required to constitute decent table manners. It is not necessary for everyone to adopt the same posture, recite precisely the same personal devotions (out of yet another formal little book), all at the same time.

I would not labour the dressy aspect except to add that the dark pin-stripes will come out on Sundays whatever I say, and that it is nothing short of tragedy when, more than once in my experience, very early weekday celebrations have been ill attended because men would not approach the altar in dungarees. It is even worse in the evening when the working clothes are dirtier.

Fifthly and finally, following E. L. Mascall, it is not sufficient to participate regularly in the Eucharist, with its unequal stress on individuality and formalism; rather we have to be eucharistic people. We have to live perpetually in the eucharistic context and this means preparation in the form of constant attempts to resolve the underlying paradoxes involved. The cosmic and the local, with stress on the former because the contemporary balance veers strongly towards the other side. Then the corporate and the personal, for the same reasons in the same order, and the immanent–transcendent balance which boils down to an application of the doctrine of the Blessed Trinity: which says it all.

There is nothing here in contradiction to more usual studies. The three-fold pattern of the Eucharist is still there: a subjective acceptance of the ministry of the Word; covenant obedience – 'All that the Lord has spoken we will do, and we will be obedient . . . Behold the blood of the covenant which the Lord has made with you . . .' (Exodus 24.7–8). Then encounter with the living Lord sacramentally present, all consummated in adoring communion as we recognize our baptismal incorporation into the sacred humanity of Jesus. An offering to the Father, through the Son, in the Spirit.

12
Finale

On 28 July 1985 I preached my farewell sermon in Truro Cathedral. Following my principle, or prejudice, against trying to combine preaching with print I do not intend to reproduce that sermon. But its substance might form a fitting conclusion to a Lent book, especially when it is realized that although Lent comes to its conclusion, giving way to the wonderfully different emphases of Eastertide, it is to be hoped that the fruits of our lenten exercises will remain, flowing into a more expansive, revivified life of prayer thereafter.

Not only was this a farewell sermon after a ten-year ministry in Truro, it was also a conclusion to forty years of ministry in all sorts of unlikely places. Before my ordination in 1946 I remember being asked by the Bishop about my aspirations, even ambitions, for the future. It was an outrageous question before ordination to which Dean Eric Abbott more healthily referred as the 'great surrender'. I lacked the courage to inform the Bishop of the rules for the discernment of spirits, that newly ordained deacons ought not to have aspirations and plans, let alone ambitions. However diplomacy prevailed and I expressed a warming towards incumbency of one country parish for the rest of my life. It showed that I too was not quite clear about the discernment of spirits, yet somehow I felt that I was not entirely on the wrong track. The Church today might reflect on the traditional principle that stability is virtuous and mobility, if not always sinful, is generally sterile. We are back to the devil who cannot keep still.

However it did not work out like that because, however deaf I was to the divine leading, it seems as if God had other ideas, and my full entry in Crockford makes it clear that no senior colleague or Christian community could put up with me for more than a year or two.

On reflection, however, I must look towards some ideal of stability which is independent of physical movement; being clearly of Benedictine *attrait* could I, looking back over forty

years, discover some guiding principle, some anchor of conviction, which gave some sort of pattern or form to my long,
harum-scarum life ministry? Here, there and everywhere;
writing, lecturing, tutoring, spiritual directing, pastoral work in
country villages and country towns, in the industrial Midlands
and affluent suburbs: what does it all add up to? What have I
been trying to do? Where is the stable, consistent core of the
thing?

My one overriding conviction through it all is easy to state and
difficult to explain. If I stand for anything it is the *absolute priority
of prayer*. State that in any context or audience and it will be
greeted with a devout nodding of heads, a polite assent, even
mild applause, because nobody, not the most outgoing
evangelist, or the most activist Christian socialist, the most self-
confessed Pelagian, dare deny it. The trouble is that only a tiny
minority believe it, or at least act upon their conviction, and
these are regarded as an impractical lunatic fringe.

St Paul insisted that everything should be done decently and
in order, and some of the foregoing analogies of the Church
have shown how this necessitates a sane administrative
structure. The parish treasurer and the grave-digger have their
essential place in the *worship* of the Body of Christ, not merely in
its maintenance. But there can be no excuse for our appalling
bureaucracy, which is only corporate Pelagianism thinly
disguised.

I was not intending to be facetious when I once suggested that
the agenda for the next session of General Synod, and possibly
for every alternate session, should be a blank sheet of paper.
How creative it would be if every other session were conducted
in complete silence, for how can one speak seriously about the
guidance of the Holy Spirit if he is never listened to? Or is the
guidance of the Spirit a rubber stamp to back up a majority
opinion? or even to support a personal prejudice? Councils and
synods have always been a necessary part of ecclesiastical
administration, not least in the formulation of doctrine, but
traditionally the paradox has also been accepted that democracy
is basically anti-trinitarian: the Father has to be *obeyed* according
to covenant, the Son encountered and, first and foremost,
adored; only then the Holy Spirit might be humbly listened to.
Yet we seem to have run away with the idea that the Peter

Principle is a dogmatic method invented by the first bishop of Rome.

I have said that the absolute Priority of Prayer is a principle easy to state but difficult to explain. The problem is made worse because the Priority of Prayer becomes a pious phrase and no more; hence the devout murmurings and nodding heads. It is ironical that the study of ascetical theology, or 'spirituality' as it has come to be called, is becoming more and more popular amongst a growing minority, yet academically, pastorally, and within ordination training, it remains a fringe subject. It also remains a subject, even a minor one, in a long list of other isolatable subjects, instead of an overall approach or application to theology as a whole. Prayer is simply Christian life in action, inevitably leading into practical service, but such service without prayer degenerates into humanism, moralism, or worse.

It is also ironical that, given this continuing taste for studies in spirituality, parochial prayer, even in the more enthusiastically proficient parish, is seen as simplistic and peripheral. The parish prayer-group is usually confined to intercession and petition, and we have seen that, important as this is in its proper place and proportion, asking favours of God or anyone else is barely discourse, conversation, the dialogue underpinning a permanent relationship.

Even when we get down to 'quiet days', or full-flown retreats, they all too easily degenerate into instruction in prayer not praying. There is too much talking from a conductor, and often other hindrances, like reading and music, as well.

Throughout this book we have tried to look at the total life of prayer in a wider and deeper sense, but what accounts for this notorious parochial gap? I suspect that the nodding heads, signifying devout acceptance of the theory of the Primacy of Prayer, harbour ingrained fears and prejudice – perhaps subconsciously, perhaps instilled by certain inherent Anglican weaknesses.

It is obvious and incontestable that God dispenses his gifts with generous diversity and bewildering disproportion. People's capacity for prayer, even the initial taste for things of the spirit, varies enormously; to be brutally blunt, some solid and mature Christians are better at it than others. But prejudice precludes us from facing the facts, we are terrified of the implications of our diversity of gifts. In all human activities and vocation, be they music, sport, commerce, art or academics, there is a hierarchy of ability; some are good, some bad, and there's an infinite range of quality in between. But so soon as this universal principle is applied to prayer, as it must be, Anglicans become very worried indeed. There must be no 'élite', but there is, and what on earth is wrong with it? In fact there would be everything wrong without it. The scratch golfer and the twenty-four handicap rabbit get on perfectly well together in the clubhouse bar after the game.

To return to our cricket analogy, the Body of Christ analogy, all Christians have their God-given place in the team, all have their proper part to play, the administrator and the mystic, the vocational intercessor and the organist. Prayer is incumbent upon all, but in vastly different modes and qualities. All are part of the local team, and ultimately it is the team that matters most, but the practical element is there to serve and support the spiritually gifted, who form the heart, soul and spearhead of the whole. What a nightmarish team without its stars. This absurd Anglican sensibility cannot erase the doctrine of the faithful Remnant from pretty well every page of the Bible, and if it tried there would be hardly any Bible left. The church local might do with a few more members, but its real need is for a few saints.

The faithful in a healthy parish – wardens, sidesmen, treasurer, ringers and so on – get on well enough together in mutual fellowship, until they are joined by widow Winifred, who is known to spend several hours a day in prayer. Her presence is something of an embarrassment, she is a little odd. Yet the prior task, and the most joyful task, of all the rest ought to be to support her and rejoice in her gifts.

I have spent forty years studying ascetical theology, and trying to apply it in pastoral practice, with whatever little success. But a constant experience, almost another nightmare, is for excellent young priests, fulfilling a creative ministry, telephoning in panic because they have discovered widow Winifred – there is bound to be at least one in every community – who is, guess what, praying. What on earth is to be done about it? Not only are we faced with the admitted subtleties of spiritual direction, but with an attempt to fit widow Winifred into the rest of the team. If we are not careful we might end up with an élite!

My unashamed hope and prayer is that some readers of this book will be led to discover, with courage, humility and joy, that they too are among the élite, fulfilling a God-given vocation. The perennial need is two-fold: a few dirty, sinful, penitent, naked Magdalens, and some nice clean-aproned Marthas with the humility to rejoice in their vital but secondary service.

The second Anglican phobia is a tacit rejection of the supernatural, which is yet another facet of Pelagianism. Prayer remains the instigator of practice, Christian life is fulfilled in service, but such service is the end of the process not the beginning. Or, to put it the other way round, prayer is the most potent power, the most practical thing there is. Screwtape-like distortion rises to the surface again, because serving others, helping the afflicted, loving one's neighbour, difficult as all that can be, is really a soft option compared with the underlying struggle against wickedness in the supernatural realm. Prayer is the explosive that shoots the gun that kills the problem, and the practical gun is singularly useless without it. But let us opt for a humanist ethic and leave the supernatural alone; to modern Anglicanism it is too difficult and too dangerous. The difficulty within the Thomist football league is that we are tempted to leave out half the world we inhabit, the first and second divisions.

Coupled with this distortion is the now fashionable emphasis on the divine immanence to the disparagement of transcendence. We shall never get the trinitarian balance exactly right, and fashions change, but reaction against eighteenth-century deism has gone too far. The charismatic movement of today and the Jesus cult of yesterday are in themselves healthy enough, another necessary reaction against a pathological fear of all emotion, against religious experience – 'enthusiasm' as it used to be called.

Love for the sacred humanity of Jesus, bold recognition of the presence of the Holy Spirit the Comforter, has always to be balanced by the terrifying reality of God the Father Almighty.

Yes, let us give loving care to that beautiful little Saxon church in rural Cornwall, let it be cleaned and polished and bedecked with early Cornish daffodils at Easter; then may we delete all those awkward bloodier bits of the psalms, not to mention the even bloodier Old Testament episodes. Let us worship the undivided Trinity in the lovely little Saxon church, not forgetting 'how dreadful is this place, for this is the very house of God, and this is the gate of heaven'.

It has not always been so in our tradition. Read and ponder any collection of Anglican seventeenth-century sermons and nine out of ten, or possibly ten out of ten, will be either directly or obliquely concerned with death. There will also be much about sin, as distinct from ethics, but with no trace of morbidity. It is all about the world to come which is also the spiritual realm in the present. Our Anglican Fathers acknowledged the glory of the eternal Trinity without fear or distortion. Today we are less happy about God the majestic Creator, it can be a frightening notion, so let us settle for gentle Jesus and the Comforter.

We have still not solved the problem of spiritual power, which remains a theological stumbling block and an historical certainty. The Priority of Prayer only makes sense when we mean prayer in all of its rich diversity and fullness, which includes but goes far beyond simple, direct intercession. It is none other than response to baptismal incorporation in Christ; spiritual power is Christ's power operating through our obedience in encounter with him. But how does it work? History simply tells us that it does.

England was converted to the faith when St Augustine of Canterbury arrived on the island of Thanet with forty companions. They might have offered service and they probably preached, but they certainly settled down to Benedictine stability and contemplated God. That is one out of thousands of examples of the mystical process of spiritual power. It is mysterious but indisputable.

When we look at our contemporary trouble spots, at violence in the inner cities, at racial hatred, or torture, murder and rape, I can muster little faith in the efficacy of 'praying about it'. I have absolute confidence in the efficacy of planting a contemplative community in the middle of it and letting God manifest his power. Prayer, real prayer, is no last resort but the first priority.

Meanwhile we submit to a sort of spiritual-pastoral schizophrenia. The Magdalens and widow Winifreds are made to feel useless, because the rest of the community seem to think they are. Yet deep down, with deep humility, the Magdalens and widow Winifreds have an eradicable hunch that they are the heart and soul of the whole show; the élite in fact. While also deep down the practical majority have an uncomfortable feeling that the Magdalens and Winifreds really are the élite, and necessarily so.

We badly need in the local church the team spirit that flourishes so healthily in the cricket pavilion and golf club. The Priority of Prayer means that prayer only issues in loving service, and that practicalities in parish life are only there to support its prayer.

There are diversities of gifts within the unity of the Body, there are comely and less comely members, but in the end it is the whole Body which constitutes the redemptive organism, because it is the Body of the Redeemer.

Cowley Publications is a work of the Society of St. John the Evangelist, a religious community for men in the Episcopal Church. The books we publish are a significant part of our ministry, together with the work of preaching, spiritual direction, and hospitality. Our aim is to provide books that will enrich their readers' religious experience and challenge it with fresh approaches to religious concerns.